Let's Get Civil

In The

Workplace

Cover Design © 2016 Martina Carroll-Garrison

Let's Get Civil In The Workplace

ISBN-13: 978-1523656523

2nd Edition

© 2016

(Previously published as The Age Of Civility)

MARTINA CARROLL-GARRISON

Owner

Workplace Civility Matters©

WWW.WorkplaceCivilityMatters.com

and

MCG Consulting Group

INFO@MCGConsultingGroup.com

Prologue

When you are at work, and you encounter a jerk or meet an uncivil person - what is the first thing you think? I usually think to myself *"OMG .....what a jerk!"* You might have another name for this nuisance or pugnacious colleague. However, because this book is an aspirational journey towards creating a civil workplace we will refrain from using any other pejorative terms or nasty names here.

Beginning with the idea that work has independent value for the worker, beyond the basics of shelter, subsistence, and survival, we can declare that each worker aspires to perform his work in harmony with his surroundings and his fellow workers. Unfortunately, regardless of the trade or the profession, it is not a common truth that today's workplace offers such harmony to every worker.

Uncivil behaviors found within the greater society have taken hold within the contemporary workplace. ***Let's Get Civil In The Workplace*** was inspired by the stories of the many thousands of worklife warriors we all have encountered in our careers. In fact, many of you have shared your stories with me as your executive leadership coach and corporate trainer, and I have been privy to the resulting damage caused to both individuals and to organizations. Together we have delved into the morass that is workplace incivility and examined the impact that uncivil behaviors have upon our workplaces and within our work lives. We have come to understand the emotional, professional, social, and spiritual toll that workplace incivility has on each of us at a very personal level, as well as on our work family and friends. For each of us who have witnessed or endured a worklife disrupted by uncivil behavior this book serves as our declaration of war. We are no longer willing to accept workplace incivility in our businesses and organizations! We are throwing down the gauntlet and declaring that we choose workplace civility over a workplace dominated by uncivil behavior! We aspire to *Let's Get Civil In The Workplace.*

As a leader practitioner, leadership consultant, and an executive coach, I serve my profession from a philosophical perspective where we each aspire to a worklife of personal fulfillment, of autonomy, and with professional mastery over our craft. Some among us also aspire to achieve a sense of purpose, perhaps even a sense of belonging to something greater than ourselves. However, the presence of workplace incivility within our work life detracts from and even sabotages our professional aspirations and our sense of belonging. That said, we now declare that we aspire to a worklife and workplace defined by civility. Although we accept that this perspective is aspirational, we will begin the journey with the end in sight, which is that we intend to *Let's Get Civil In The Workplace* now!

Contents

Part One: Workplace Incivility Sucks!

Part Two: 40 Keys To Civility

Part Three: A Corporate Strategy For Civility

Part One: Workplace Incivility Sucks!

1. And So It Began...

Welcome To The New Job!

It was a typical gray winter day that greeted Chuck Rice as he emerged upwards from the underground of the Washington, D.C. Metro system and onto the cold streets of Northeast D.C. It was the first day of his dream job with an incredible organization that enjoyed international acclaim. It was one of those organizations where everyone felt that they belonged to something much greater than themselves.

Chuck Rice had been poached from another organization and felt very fortunate with his new employment opportunity. Having alighted from the D.C. underground into the cold morning sunshine, Chuck observed that everybody seemed to be walking with a sense of energy, of purpose, and direction, and everybody was carrying a cup of coffee. This was a new visual for Chuck, and as he was so excited about his new assignment that he found himself absorbing every detail of this new life. He wanted to make sure that he fit in with his new organization, and the people he would be working with, and that he would hit the ground running.

Chuck figured that if becoming a successful part of the new group meant carrying a cup of coffee everywhere, then it would be a good idea to stop by Starbucks and buy some. He began what would become an expensive morning ritual as he ordered that first cup of java. The hustle of the coffee shop was exciting for Chuck as he witnessed the efficiency of the baristas asking names, taking orders, making coffee, toasting sandwiches, delivering orders, collecting money, and then starting all over again. Having added cream and milk and sugar, and observing everybody else's coffee ritual in the coffee shop, Chuck continued to make his way to his new office. His heart pounding a little bit faster than normal, his excitement level slightly more elevated than his normal reserved self, and his overall joy at the idea of starting to work on the new project for this prestigious organization visibly shining through on his face, in his smile, and in the twinkle in his eyes.

Chuck knew where he was going and how to get into the building and even how get to the floor of his office. He knew where his desk was as he'd gone through a very thorough orientation with the H.R. folks and his onboarding sponsor the week before. During the interview process, Chuck believed he had gleaned a very clear brief of what his new assignment was to be, and why he had been poached from his previous employer. Chuck had successfully mastered this type of project previously, although on a much smaller scale. He knew the secret to his success was based upon his ability to build consensus, network, create relationships, and define and execute a win-win strategy for all the parties in the transaction. Chuck was very excited about the growth opportunity offered by this new job, and very excited about the caliber of the team he had been given to lead. He was equally excited about the executive capacity of the senior leadership team he would be reporting to, and the professional opportunity offered by being exposed to their coaching, teaching, and mentoring.

In hindsight, day one of his new job was a bit of a blur as Chuck went about meeting his team of first reports and sharing his philosophy. His goal was simple, to understand the lay of the land and learn about his team and the resources that were available to him. The next several days were quite similar as he reached out beyond his immediate team and met with his counterparts and peers, and other stakeholders in the organization to whom he would either need support from or would be supporting in the execution of their operation. Chuck figured he had a week to understand the lay of the land and get a feel for how things worked. As expected, the senior leader for his organization, the Big Guy, scheduled a chat on the afternoon of Friday of the first week. Chuck prepared and readied for the conversation. The same senior leader was the one who actively recruited and ultimately selected Chuck for the position. Chuck felt very privileged to have such a high-ranking patron within the organization, especially as the Big Guy was a well know figure in their industry and appeared to have significant influence.

Friday afternoon came, and Chuck made his way to the rarefied air of the 15th floor where the Big Guy sat. Naturally it was a well-lit and large corner office. Furnished with what seemed to be solid oak furniture, tomes of important leather-bound books on massive bookshelves, and a heavily adorned I-Love-Me-Wall. The wall was ensconced with framed diplomas, degrees, letters of appreciation from significant persons in their industry, and other regalia that reflected the Big Guy's personal success and professional achievements. Chuck had seen such monuments before, and understood that this was a necessary calling card to announce to those who didn't know that they are in the presence of greatness. Chuck sat in a leather bound chair, basking in the glow of his professional satisfaction with where he found himself on this late Friday afternoon, on a cold winter's day in Washington, D.C.

As the meeting began Chuck prepared himself to be in a listening mode. Although he had done his due diligence regarding the lay of the land during the several days preceding this meeting, he was fully prepared to receive the Big Guys perspective on the assignment he was hired for. Chuck's expectation was that the conversation would be a reiteration of the brief that was outlined during the interview process. Chuck sat in his chair feeling very confident that he had made the right decision in accepting this job, with this organization, and especially in working with the Big Guy. To Chuck's astonishment (he could not overstate his astonishment) the Big Guy began the conversation by saying that the other organization to which they needed to partner with *"...were a bunch of dickheads."*

Chuck blinked (and mentally gasped)! He was not quite certain that he heard what he just thought that he had heard. It wasn't that he was unfamiliar with the derogatory term, rather he was astonished that the Big Guy, as a senior executive and influential leader, would use such a pejorative term to describe fellow professionals in their industry. Chuck was especially dismayed because the Big Guy was talking about the organization that they needed to partner with to execute the mission that Chuck had been hired for. As Chuck listened to the Big Guy describe his perspective of this other organization, and to the tone and tenor in describing the working relationship, he wondered why he had never picked up on any of this animosity or disdain during the series of interviews leading to his accepting this job offer.

Over the weekend, Chuck replayed the conversation in his head many times. He realized that it was not a conversation, merely a one-sided diatribe about the failings of other organization. Cognitive dissonance besieged his thoughts, as he could not reconcile his first perception of both the organization and the Big Guy with the conversation that he had been privy to that Friday evening on the 15th floor of his new office building. Unfortunately, the attitude and behavior of the Big Guy, which Chuck observed during their first chat, was not a momentary lapse of professional etiquette. Over the next several months Chuck observed and endured many such displays of invective, disdain, and animosity about and towards their partner organization. The consequence of this behavior, exercised openly by the Big Guy, contaminate almost all of his colleagues, and echoed throughout their organization.

Somebody Is Always Watching....

The culture, beliefs, and values, of any organization, business enterprise, or work group, is shaped by the **worst behavior** that the leader is willing to put up with!

Acts of workplace incivility serve as the lowest common denominator for establishing culture and organizational behavior.

Somebody Is Always Watching

Almost every employee that predated Chuck's hiring wore the same mantle of disdain, and spoke the same venom about their partner organization as did the Big Guy. In fact, those who spoke it more virulently than others appeared to curry greater favor and approval from the Big Guy. Not only was the relationship with the other organization severely damaged and untenable, but also the spirals of incivility from the 15th floor had wreaked havoc in Chuck's own team too.

Chuck came to realize that he found himself working for a pariah organization, which was as uncivil in its internal relationships as it was to its external stakeholders. From Chuck's perspective, the sustaining source of the animosity and the subsequent incivility within the organization emanated from with the Big Guy. Professionally, Chuck began to feel isolated, as he knew this was not a problem he could fix. He understood that the secret to his previous success was based upon his ability to build consensus, to network, to create relationships and to define and execute a win-win strategy for all the parties in the transaction. However this approach was not possible now. It was clear that this was not the job Chuck signed up for.

Mental Stress

Chuck the professional was not alone in his distress, Chuck the man was also distraught. His personal and physical self was distressed by the situation within which he found himself. Chuck had enough workplace experience to be able to recognize that power can force compliance, which explained how the behavior of the Big Guy influenced the behavior of almost everyone else in the organization. However, Chuck's preference for a culture of cooperation and consensus and civility was at odds with the culture within which he found himself. Chuck understood that he could not be true to himself in an environment where disrespect is the predominant currency, as he knew that this type of behavior damages support necessary in all crucial situations. The culture was damaged and his colleagues failed to share important information or withheld their effort or resources. Chuck was also aware enough to understand that intermittent stressors, such as experiencing or witnessing acts of incivility, (or even recalling them over the weekend while away from work) would elevate his level of stress hormones, possibly leading to a host of health problems, including the risk of a cardiovascular disease.

Chuck weighed his options and determined that he must pursue alternative employment consistent with his need for a civil and respectful culture and work environment, and one where he believed he could build consensus towards group and organizational success.

2. What Is This Behavior We Speak Of?

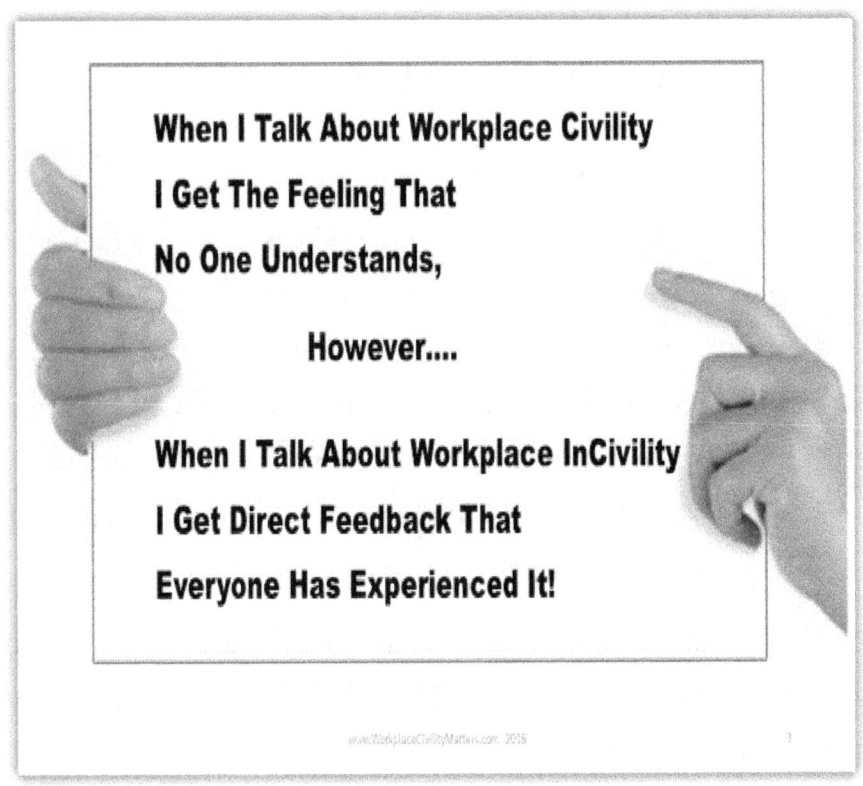

**When I Talk About Workplace Civility
I Get The Feeling That
No One Understands,**

However....

**When I Talk About Workplace InCivility
I Get Direct Feedback That
Everyone Has Experienced It!**

When I Talk About Civility....

How does workplace civility differ from other cultural norms in the workplace? What are the rules? Can it be taught? What particular aspects of the workplace and our worklife are impacted by knowing about workplace civility? How does an organization respond to uncivil behavior? Is your workplace expectation of civil behavior at odds with contemporary cultural behaviors outside the workplace? This book will address these various questions and identify ways to imbue and instill civility within the organization and across the workforce, from the C-Suite to the shop floor.

The Road Less Travelled...

A myriad of research confirms that there is a very real cost to workplace incivility, both to individuals and organizations. Regardless of whether you are part of a small workgroup or belong to a national organization, fostering workplace civility as a cultural norm will increase morale, facilitate cultural competence, encourage effective communication, decrease turnover, boost service-orientation, sustain high performance, and even enhance your organizations' external reputation with stakeholders.

Workplace civility can also positively impact the bottom line. Who would not want this type of worklife? The problem is that in many workplaces we have unknowingly slipped into a culture of incivility and don't know that there is a way to change it.

Workplace civility is both an organizational issue and an individual issue. My goal for this book (now a 2nd edition), is twofold; to build the argument and instill the idea that workplace civility is a pillar of effective organizational behavior, and that workplace civility is a required leadership competency. In the space between a concerted organizational commitment and the development of individual capacity for civil behavior there is the opportunity to make a substantial improvement in the culture of your organization.

Research supports that when both organizations and individuals embrace the idea that workplace civility is an expected organizational behavior and a required leadership competency, we can begin to turn the tide on deviant workplace behaviors and adverse cultures; which undermine the wellbeing of our employees and colleagues, and detract from the goals of high performing organizations.

In Part One of the book we explore the rise of the phenomenon of workplace incivility against the backdrop of changing social behaviors, changing levels of interpersonal trust, changing workplaces, and the changing expectations placed upon workers. Upon establishing the cause of workplace incivility we then explore the alternative, which is the preferred working situation.

In Part Two of the book we have included a wide variety of workplace and worklife strategies, which we examine through the lens of either deviant (uncivil) or positive (civil) workplace behaviors. This book is intended as a 'how-to' guide for leaders, managers, influencers, high performing individuals, corporate trainers, and human resource professionals. The material is designed to assist those who want to understand the impact of workplace incivility, and develop a foundation upon which to build and promote civility as a preferred organizational value.

Before proceeding however we must acknowledge and thank the many civility researchers who have gone before us on this road less travelled. Regarding the subject of workplace civility, many other great minds, academics, and worklife practitioners have also researched and written about the subject. Suffice to say that this book affirms our debt of gratitude to many other scholars, and that we have drawn from and built upon their research and wisdom.

In researching the phenomenon of workplace incivility we became aware that the antithesis is workplace civility. The pursuit and sustainment of the model for a civil workplace has now become our professional passion. Through the coaching process, we have observed firsthand how individual clients wrestle with the insidious nature of workplace incivility and its outcomes, and strive to become more civil themselves, while also imbuing civility as a cultural norm within their organization.

3. Imbue Civility As A Cultural Norm

Workplace Civility Is Both An Organizational Issue And An Individual Issue

We each are in pursuit of our own civil workplace. ***Let's Get Civil In The Workplace*** reflects aspirational behaviors for ourselves as worklife practitioners, as well as for other workplace warriors who may be challenged by the demands of their daily grind. We know too well that perceived injustice, work exhaustion, and job dissatisfaction are just some of the components that may influence employees to exhibit rude, discourteous behaviors in the workplace.

We have all been confronted with worklife situations that may not bring forth our best behaviors or our highest and best selves. Unfortunately, we can all attest that within our worklife we have sometimes succumbed to the voice of our baser self. Perhaps this happens in response to the frustration brought about by ambiguous direction, idiotic business processes, inane stupidity, or limited resources to name just a few challenges. We allow these situations to justify why we behave uncivilly to our fellow workplace warriors.

In workshops across the country where we have presented the Workplace Civility Matters© program, we typically begin by admitting that most likely we will not be presenting entirely new information to many of the workshop participants. However, the feedback is almost unanimous, which is that the workshop topic around workplace civility is a great reminder and a welcome discussion. Often we find that the training topic is one that has been longed for by the workgroup, although they did not have a specific name for it. We have come to understand that within the organizational worklife where the organizations culture is unhealthy, the topic of workplace civility is one that needs a forum, or place at the table, in addition to becoming a chapter in the organizations' leadership training curricula.

In *Let's Get Civil In The Workplace,* we propose that the pursuit of workplace civility is an organizational response to the presence of deviant behaviors, and a desire to achieve positive cultural norms. At its core, the programmed pursuit of a civil workplace involves two steps:

- The first step depends on whether organizations and individuals are open to accepting the presence of and the insidious impact of uncivil behaviors.

- The second step depends on whether the same organizations and individuals then commit to new ways of thinking and behaving; Step two is further contingent upon whether a critical mass of these individuals within the organization can accept the value of adapting together and holding each other accountable for acquiring a positive culture within their organization.

Hopefully this book will contribute to new knowhow for those employees yearning for a constructive discussion around the concept of a civil workplace, a positive culture, and the values of citizenship we each hold dear.

As a final thought, we offer a coaching insight, which is that through the process of reading this book we encourage you to reflect on the information presented. Even when the ideas presented are not new to you, we suggest that you reflect with a new awareness and understanding of your own thought processes around how your current behavior can contribute unconsciously to the presence of incivility or civility within your organization.

4. The Dawn Of Workplace Incivility

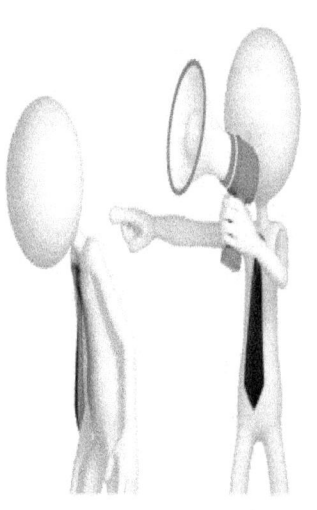

Incivility And Poor Workplace Culture Suck The Happiness Out Of Our Workday
(... so what is it???)

✓ ... bad behavior

✓ ... disrespectful treatment of others...

✓ ... bullying

✓ ... petty theft

✓ ... emotional abuse

✓ ... public shaming

✓ ... professional humiliation

✓ ... social isolation

www.WorkplaceCivilityMatters.com 2016

Aspects Of Incivility

In ***Let's Get Civil In The Workplace,*** we declare that this is the day we fight! Today, in picking up this book we challenge you to face down the workplace enemy that is incivility, and replace it with the values that you hold dear, including the values of civility towards and among your fellow workplace warriors.

Charles Handy (1990) noted in *The Age of Unreason* that *"...the future we predict today is not inevitable. We can influence it, if we know what we want it to be..."* We can and should be in charge of our own destinies in a time of change. So how is it then that we find ourselves in the latter part of the second decade of the 21st century where we are immersed in a world where civility in politics, in social media, and most especially in the workplace is lacking? Although Handy predicted the changing nature of work, the first seeds of incivility in the workplace were sewn with the dehumanizing advent of the industrial revolution. We lost workplace civility when we lost the value we placed upon the individual craftsman and his contribution to his community.

We begin telling the story of *Let's Get Civil In The Workplace* by remembering an earlier era when labor was honorable and the laborer was honored. There was a time in our recent past when the craftsman was revered for his work as he produced finished products such as tool, clothes, and glassware. Traveling forward in time the factory replaced the artisan and employees performed repetitive functions from sunup to sundown, without ever being responsible for the final product. No longer did the craftsman enjoy the accolades of having created a useful tool, as he had become a simple cog in the production line on the factory floor. We can understand how incivility has become both the norm in our society and within the workplace when the craftsman was no longer a valued citizen.

5. Four Social Foci Have Evolved

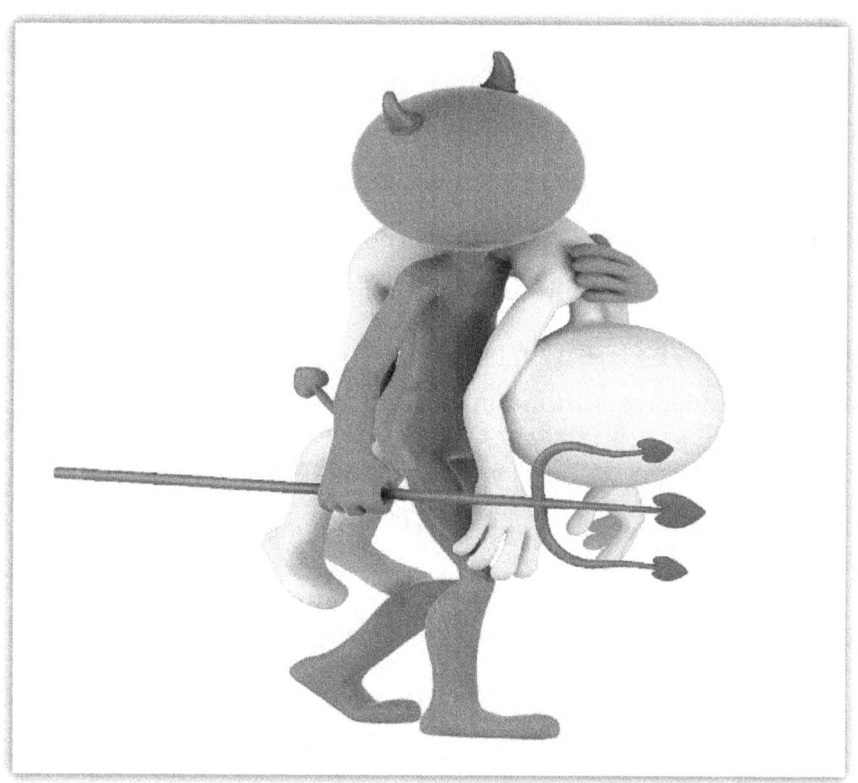

Causes Of Incivility

There appears to be four social foci that have evolved to support the prevalence of workplace incivility as a fixture within our work lives. These foci include (1) declining social behaviors, (2) declining interpersonal trust, (3) a changing workplace, and (4) a changing worker. This brings us to where we are today, which as

Handy predicted in *The Age of Unreason*, is an environment fraught with change. As the societal and organizational changes and pressures mount we as individual worklife practitioners and workgroups have succumbed to lessor versions of ourselves, and allowed incivility to permeate our work lives.

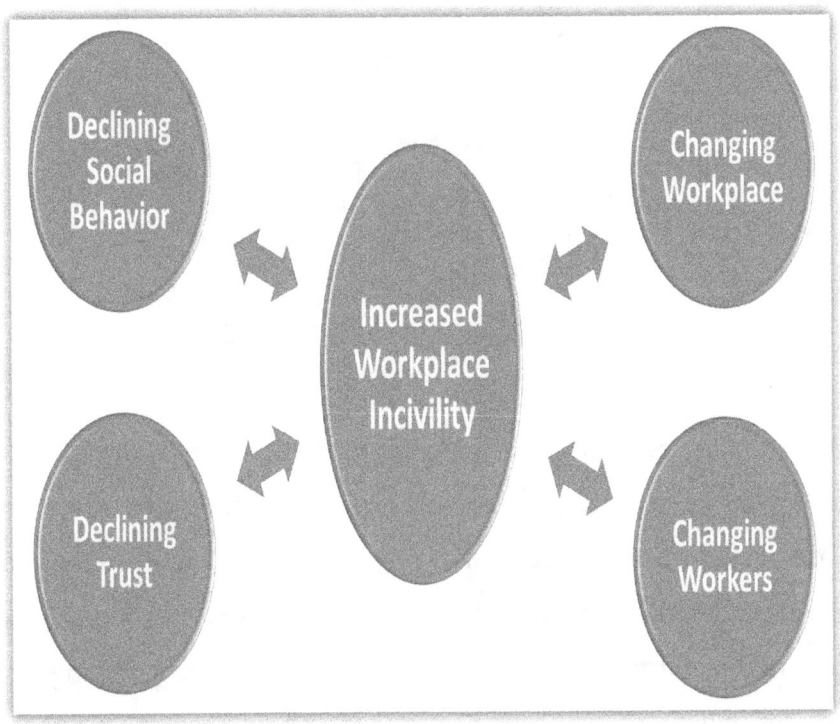

The Four Foci Of Incivility

#1: Declining Social Behaviors

Social behaviors in contemporary society are changing and not for the better. We are exposed to a daily tirade of news reports about acts of violence, incivility, deviance, corruption, and meanness. While we can offer numerous research studies about declining social behaviors to support this assertion, it is simpler to consider what the major news outlets report on any given day. Contemporary society is a defacto warzone, as we are inundated by reports of daily acts of social deviance and incivility. However, the question that has to be asked is whether this is our new normal or is it a blip in the general evolutionary process of mankind, or the specific advancement or decline of our civilization? While we would rather believe that today's social behaviors are a blip they are still very troubling.

By way of example on 1 December 2015, the headline news page for MSN.com (http://www.msn.com/en-us/news?ocid=sk2cdhp) presented over 40 instances of deviant social issues that reflect the current condition of our modern society. Unfortunately, the negative social behaviors addressed as front page news are not solely the purview of MSN.com, as each of these articles were collected from other global news sources, including the Washington Post, Reuters, The Associated Press, and a variety of local news outlets. We are bombarded daily with stories of social deviance, including crime, corruption and a variety of other actions and behaviors that violate our senses and represent deviant social norms. The good news is perhaps that we are still incensed by these frequent behaviors and do not accept them as being acceptable. We understand that social norms are rules and expectations by which members of our society are conventionally guided, whereas social deviance is an absence of conformity to these norms. Research suggests that the frothy acts of deviant behavior reported in the news reflect an absence of conformity to our preferred social norms.

The reference to these forty articles serves to illustrate the abundance of issues we are confronted with on a daily basis. With the advent of numerous television channels offering 24-hour news coverage, as well as news delivered on the Internet and through smart phones, the possibility to be constantly in contact with the news outlets has increased dramatically. Regardless of whether media outlets sensationalize deviant social behaviors to increase sales, the number of antisocial events reported on any given day are overwhelming and eventually make inroads into our social consciousness. Although the impact that media exposure has on individuals is understudied, intuitively we can accept that the constant barrage of negative news takes its toll on all of us and causes us stress reactivity.

#2: Lack Of Trust In Our Modern Society

The lack of trust in our modern society underpins many of today's social ailments. As coaches and corporate trainers, we have long observed that trust is a necessary component of effective working relationships. However, trust as a societal value appears to be in short supply. The presence of trust is hugely significant within a civil society, as social scientists have informed us that it helps people work together for the common good. Trust breaks down barriers and encourages support among and between people, especially those from different religious beliefs, political ideologies, cultures, and socioeconomic backgrounds. In contrast, a lack of trust or the exercise of distrustful behaviors among and between people and groups encourages meanness and incivility.

Without attempting to explain the why of why societal trust has diminished, we believe we can each reflect upon our own lives and perhaps begin to acknowledge the reality of our distrust for others. Regardless of our own personal perception of the decline in societal trust however, there are several recent surveys and polls that support this emerging truth. Trust in our fellow humans is eroding and various surveys confirm we have become increasingly distrustful of others in recent years.

A 2014 Pew Survey on social trends found that as the Millennial generation have arrived into adulthood, and by default into the workplace, they expressed significantly lower social trust than their earlier counterparts. The survey found that only 19 percent of Millennials indicate that they trust other people, whereas 31 percent of Gen Xers, 40 percent of Baby Boomers, and 37 percent of the Greatest Generation say that people can be trusted.

An Associated Press GfK poll conducted in 2013 had similar findings to the Pew survey, and reflected that most Americans are suspicious of each other in even the most basic of our daily interactions. Less than one-third have trust in the strangers they meet when traveling, or the store clerk who swipes their credit cards, or even other drivers on the road. Significantly, only a third of those surveyed said they thought most people could be trusted, whereas in 1972, half of adults surveyed said others were trustworthy. In the past forty years we have seen that trust as a social value has declined.

However, it appears not just to be a societal condition, as research also shows that Americans don't fully trust their family members either. According to a World Values Survey, only 69 percent of Americans report that they trust their family members *"completely."* While this number is higher than our level of trust for non-family members, we are close to the bottom of the graph of the numerous countries surveyed. While Middle Eastern and Central European countries are at the top, family trust was reported to be lower than the US only in Ghana, Lebanon, Azerbaijan and the Netherlands. We know that trust adds to the presence of civility within a civil society, while, the presence of distrustful behaviors encourages meanness and incivility within our society. With the decline of trust in the larger society is it any wonder then that we endure incivility in our workplace, which has become an extension of our home life?

#3: The Modern Workplace Has Changed

Global competition, dwindling markets, corporate outsourcing, and a rise of temporary and term employees has introduced a greater element of uncertainty into the modern workplace. The contemporary workplace mirrors the changes in society over the past four decades. Forty years ago, factories would produce the same product over and over again without needing to change either the method of production or the product. However, our interconnected world has accelerated the speed of change and therefore increased the need for companies and employees to adapt. In the last 25 years the global workplace has undergone a historic transformation, one that has signaled gigantic changes in our worklife, and in our lives in general.

The most significant change to our worklife was ushered in by the development of new information technologies, sparking greater connectivity and the emergence of the global economy. Organizational management and relationships changed as a result of geographic distances and so arose the necessity for decentralized decision-making. No longer would organizations choose centralized and hierarchical control – a system of management that endured since the era of the Ford motor car and the now infamous Ford assembly line. The geographically dispersed market place effectively changed the organization, which also brought the influence of the global market into the workplace in ways that had not previously been experienced by purely domestic operations.

Contemporary management books now speak to new flexibilities in production methods, including vertical disintegration, compartmentalization of production, and the outsourcing of work effort across the global marketplace. These emerging business paradigms are not just significant to new MBA graduates, as they also impact individual workers' lives on a global scale. The business of business and enterprise has moved away from a simple domestic or regional enterprise. Businesses are now organized and or influenced on a global scale. For example, the successor motor companies of today synchronizes component production with manufacturers from across the globe, designing automotive components in Europe, manufacturing and assembling them in Asia, and hosting the final assembly in each of the consumer countries, using nontraditional, subcontracted, term, or temporary labor.

A significant and far-reaching consequence of the move from the classic Ford assembly line method of production, where all work occurred in one plant, is that the employment relationship has changed. No longer are employees guaranteed the benefits and consistency of employment-for-life, for such was the working relationship that many of our parents enjoyed. In the United States and other developed economies, employers have moved away from a long-term relationship governed by the rules of the internal labor market, just as they moved away from a centralized managerial structure.

The casualization of the contemporary working relationship has eroded employee security and any attendant belief about the efficacy of putting others before self. Contemporary employers have moved into the realm of a short-term working relationship governed by international labor markets and a decentralized managerial structure. This transformation in the labor market has significantly affected the working relationships among and between employees and between the employee and their employer. Among other societal changes the enduring cohesiveness of workgroups, which perhaps our parents may have enjoyed, has been replaced by something that is less relationship based.

What has happened over the past 25 years, in the most simplistic of terms, is that the compulsion and the self-interest to maintain a positive long-term relationship with your colleagues and employer has been removed. In our parents era, where there may have only been one major employer in the town, there was a vested interest for each employee to set aside minor nuisances and work and play well together for the sake of the entire group. Communities grew up around factories and other major employment centers, and community trust was both valuable and necessary for effective working and living relationships.

Cohesiveness and trust were significant elements of both the working relationship and the community relationship. The decline of contemporary workplace civility is inextricably linked to the decline of societal trust in general, and the disappearance of central management systems, long-term workplace relationships, secure employment opportunities, and the associated employer-community cohesiveness and interdependence. As the social bonds established in secure employment situations have waned, we have had to adjust our perspective of others. A consequence of declining social bonds is that the decline of social trust also represents a prominent societal change. Additionally, the loosening of social bonds has resulted in our moving from the domain of "us" to the domain of "I", as we are becoming more individualistic than was the norm in our parents' generation.

#4: The Modern Worker Has Changed

The concept of individual feeling and personal affect are increasingly prominent in contemporary business organizations. The idea of feelings and emotions concerning employee interaction has a rich history of workplace research. However, there are three fairly recent developments within the domain of the contemporary workplace that will shed light into emerging changes of understanding about the individual employee within his or her workplace.

➢ The first development is the recognition and understanding that business innovation and creativity is increasingly emotion-driven.

➢ The second development is that businesses now increasingly focus on dominating employees' interpersonal interactions, as evidenced by the growth in leadership training, executive coaching, behavior expectation management, grievance handling, publication of content such as *Let's Get Civil In The Workplace,* and focused conversations around the notion of cultural norms.

➤ The third development is that employees are hired not just for what they know but for what they can create. Employees are expected to be both creative and to innovate at work. This is a substantial change in the employee-employer agreement, as the contemporary employee has moved beyond the role of a knowledge worker, and is expected to evolve his thinking in ways his predecessors never imagined. The contemporary worker is expected to be a creator of new ideas, new technologies, new processes, and new ways of looking at his role as a worker. He is also expected to be more than a knowledge worker, he is a creator of knowledge and ideas, and a stimulator of new ideas in others.

Each of these three developments creates a significant disruption in the type of worker we are becoming, as well as the way we work together. More significantly, the expectation of emotion-driven performance, stimulating employee interaction, and pushing for creation and innovation have changed the way we work with others in the workplace.

This new type of employee, namely the creator of knowledge and ideas, is significantly more valuable than his predecessor who was the knowledge worker. His individual feelings and affect are an integral part of his value proposition as well as the organizations' performance outcome equation. Today's effective employee has become more valued for his affect than his knowledge. This new employee, this creator of knowledge and ideas, can now be referred to as an affect worker.

Interpersonal affect travels faster than the speed of light. In the blink of an eye, we perceive more about those we meet than we are consciously aware of, and we respond accordingly with openness or being guarded depending upon the affect. For the new affect worker the traditional worklife boundaries have either morphed or dissolve as a result of the emergence of new information technologies. Picture the millennial marketer who is constantly on, constantly connected, constantly observing, engaging, sharing, regardless of whether he is in the worksite or in a social setting.

The traditional concept of the structured 9-to-5 work day has been redefined by the rising acceptance of flexi-time employment, casualization of employment relationships, and the creep of work-life technologies into the domain of the non-work environment. Each of these societal changes has contributed to the erosion of the distinction between the individual's personal life and his worklife identity. The personal behaviors of the non-work self now appear more frequently in the worklife. While previously this would have been wholly unacceptable, the new reality of decentralized management makes this both acceptable and welcome by the organization. The environment of ever-changing work processes now demands more of the whole person to be present in the workplace, which for the affect worker permits the bringing to the workplace the source of his creativity, adaptability, and flexibility.

Unfortunately, the effect of this change in employee distinction has a far-reaching impact on both the workplace and the workers. In expecting the affect worker to be a part of our organization, not only are we inviting a different aspect of the worker to participate in the value creation process, we are also asking each employee to also interact with, and engage with, and collaborate with, other similar organizational value creators, more specifically other affect employees. However, we don't have a clear understanding of the new rules of engagement, nor is our workforce trained to operate in this fast paced entrepreneurial, co-constructive, innovative, and creative environment.

We have changed our expectation and preference for the type of employee we want to show up in the workplace. As we have begun to move our preference from the familiar knowledge worker to the more vaguely understood affect worker, we are confronted with the dilemma of a changing work environment. We have not yet written the new rule book for expected behaviors. However, it is clear that from the viewpoint of performance outcomes, organizations must begin to invest in training that affects employees' interpersonal interactions, and how they see themselves and their role within the organization. As employers, we have the opportunity to offer coaching, teaching, and mentoring to our workforce in an attempt to shape and influence their interpersonal behaviors. When we don't take the opportunity to positively influence this aspect of our employees' behavior, the vacuum will be filled with the societal values that are already disrupting the advancement of our civilization. Employers have both a responsibility and an opportunity to stave off the advance of incivility in the workplace and perhaps push-back against the continued rise of anti-social behavior found within the greater population.

6. Gateway Behaviors And Acts Of Violence

Workplace Incivility Is Gateway Behavior To Acts Of Violence

- According to the Department of Justice, violence-related fatalities are only the tip of the iceberg
  - One million individuals become victims of violent crime each year while working or on duty.
  - Workplace violence accounts for 16% of the more than 6.5 million acts of violence experienced by individuals age 12 and over.
  - A half million employees miss 1.8 million days of work each year, resulting in more than $55 million in lost wages, not including days covered by sick and annual leave.

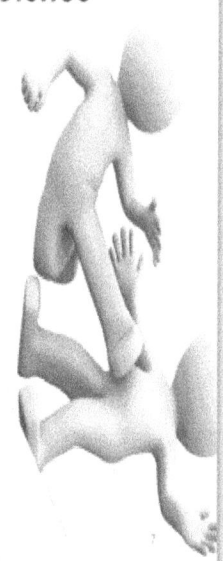

www.WorkplaceCivilityMatters.com 2016

Gateway Behaviors To Acts Of Violence

So we have established that deviant social behaviors are ever present in our daily news diet, and appear to represent a decline in the social fabric of our communities. We have also established that trust among and between the general populations is at an all-time low. We have documented that the contemporary workplace has changed beyond recognition over the past 25 years, and the social bonds that held our parents workplaces together no longer exist. We also recognize that the prized employee is no longer a knowledge worker, but an individualist worker who is prized for his personal affect and creativity.

If we believe that employers ought not to concern themselves with issues such as deviant societal behaviors, declining interpersonal trust, changes in the contemporary workplace and the modern affect worker, then we are leaving ourselves exposed. These four distinct phenomena add to diminished civility within our society, and collectively they give rise to incivility in our workplace.

We need to care about workplace incivility because we now know that acts of incivility are gateway behaviors that often escalate and cross over into violence. The tipping point occurs when workplace incivility evolves to other less ambiguous and more direct forms of deviant behaviors, such as physical aggression, violence, and even murder. The prevalence of acts of workplace incivility are widely supported by research. As significant is the prevalence of acts of violence at work, which are often preceded by acts of incivility.

The U.S. government reports that violence-related fatalities are only the tip of the iceberg. According to the Department of Justice, one million individuals become victims of violent crime each year while working or on duty. A half million employees miss 1.8 million days of work each year, resulting in more than $55 million in lost wages, not including days covered by sick and annual leave. Workplace violence accounts for 16 percent of the more than 6.5 million acts of violence experienced by individuals age 12 and over. We now understand that acts of incivility are the precursor to the 1.8 million loss days of work.[1]

As a result of changes in the relationships between personal life and worklife we can easily understand the link between the rise of uncivil behavior in society and the spillover effect on the workplace. We know that technology has created a blurred line between working hours and private time, and deviant behaviors found within our society are not constrained by the office door or the company security guard. Uncivil, rude, disruptive, and demeaning behavior among workplace professionals is representative of the behaviors found in our greater community, our schools and universities, and our social and political institutions. These antisocial behaviors, when combined with diminished trust for others, and a changing organizational landscape, as well as the evolving demands placed on the contemporary affect worker, all link together to create the workplace caldron where acts of incivility flourish. The changing dynamic of the internal workplace and external societal shifts contribute to the phenomenon of rising workplace incivility. Workplace incivility can pose a serious threat to employee

---

[1] http://www.afscme.org/news/publications/workplace-health-and-safety/fact-sheets/pdf/Workplace-Violence-Fact-Sheet.pdf

wellbeing, and can also significantly impact organizational performance and outcomes.

7. What Is Workplace Incivility?

The Big Question?

What is your understanding now of the phenomenon of workplace incivility? Were you aware of the phenomenon or the name for it before picking up this book? Did reading about the decline of social trust, or the increase of deviant social behaviors lay the foundation for a new understanding of workplace behaviors?

How does the term 'workplace incivility" affect your sense of yourself in your workplace?

We often find that many workplace warriors are familiar with the behaviors around workplace incivility, although they don't have a concrete understanding of the phenomenon, or are fully aware on the impact, or even a specific name for the behaviors. However, as soon as we list the various behaviors identified under the rubric of workplace incivility most people immediately recognize it and can attest to its presence in their worklife. The inherent ambiguity around workplace incivility is part of the problem, as most people assume the behaviors to be simply an annoyance, or a nuisance, or merely background noise within their work environment.

The several telltale signs or effects of an uncivil work environment include diminished health, decreased job satisfaction, decreased productivity, performance loss, reduced commitment, and increased employee attrition. Rude and disrespectful behavior, which violates workplace customs and norms, can also diminish positive employee attitudes, and employee propensity for learning. Simply stated, civil workplace behaviors impact organizational performance and business outcomes.

Basic Definitions And Explanations

3 Contemporary Definitions Of Incivility

1. ... *the quality or state of being uncivil*
   - Free Merriam - Webster Dictionary

2. ... *rude behavior or language: rude or impolite behavior or language*
   - Bing Dictionary

3. ... *an uncivil or discourteous act*
   - Free Online Dictionary

PEOPLE NOWADAYS

Help me!

People Nowadays....

The concept of workplace incivility is not unknown to us, yet we are often at a loss to define it or frame it within the context of our own worklife. To understand the phenomenon we can begin by examining the word 'incivility,' which is derived from the Latin *incivilis*, meaning '*not of a citizen*,' that is not a citizen by the norms of a civil society.

Incivility is the quality or state of being uncivil and it includes rude or impolite behavior or language, or an uncivil or discourteous act, or is the quality or state of being uncivil. However, to further demystify the concept let's examine three contemporary definitions of incivility from a variety of sources.

1.Incivility Is……The Quality Or State Of Being Uncivil - Free Merriam - Webster Dictionary

2.Incivility Is……Rude Behavior Or Language: Rude Or Impolite Behavior Or Language - Bing Dictionary

3.Incivility Is……An Uncivil Or Discourteous Act - Free Online Dictionary

To better understand the phenomenon of incivility it helps to examine and understand the opposite behavior, which is civility. As mentioned in the forward to this book, our research around the subject of workplace incivility and civility is built upon the earlier works of a wide variety of thought leaders and worklife commentators. Some of their words are reflected in the six definitions below and represent a broad agreement around the complex topic of civility or good citizenship.

1."Dialogic Civility Points To A Public Moral Dimension Where Exclusion Based On Gender, Race, And Ethnicity Is Rejected, While Different Voices Framed From Different Standpoints Are Encouraged To Contribute To Public Dialogue" (Arnett & Arneson)

2."Civility Is Liberating. It Frees Us From Self-Absorption, Impulse, And Mood" (Forni)

3."Fundamentally, Civility Is A Form Of Goodness Resulting From An Awareness Of Others" (Bogorad)

4. "Civility Is The Etiquette Of Democracy" (De Tocqueville)

5. "Civility Is The Ethic For Relating To The Stranger" (Carter)

6. "...Civility Is Founded On Our Experience Of A Democratic Society In Which All Citizens Are Supposed To Enjoy Fair Treatment Before The Law" (Davetian)

6 Contemporary Definitions Of Civility

1. Dialogic civility points to a public moral dimension where exclusion based on gender, race, and ethnicity is rejected, while different voices framed from different standpoints are encouraged to contribute to public dialogue Arnett & Arneson

2. Civility is liberating. It frees us from self-absorption, impulse, and mood Forni

3. Fundamentally, civility is a form of goodness resulting from an awareness of others Bogorad

4. Civility is the etiquette of democracy - de Tocqueville

5. Civility is the ethic for relating to the stranger - Carter

6. Civility is founded on our experience of a democratic society in which all citizens are supposed to enjoy fair treatment before the law – Davetian

6 Contemporary Definitions Of Civility

Our Definition Of Workplace Incivility

Workplace incivility is a

disrespectful, paltry, and mistrustful

interaction with fellow workplace and

worklife participants.

www.WorkplaceCivilityMatters.com 2018 10

Our Workplace Incivility Definition

The behaviors ascribed to Workplace Incivility include our disregard another's' basic humanity and our respective duty to care as fellow workplace warriors. Workplace incivility reflects a set of behaviors expressed towards another and has three parts; (1) Being disrespectful, (2) being paltry, (3) being mistrustful. Our working definition is that "Workplace Incivility is a disrespectful, paltry, and mistrustful interaction with fellow workplace and worklife participants".

From our research, and as observed during numerous engagements with coaching clients, the instigator of workplace incivility may intentionally or unintentionally obfuscate the nature or purpose of his acts of incivility, specifically with the intention to cause harm to the target. Stated another way, we have observed that the uncivil person may act uncivilly out of ignorance or a lack of self-awareness, or they may act uncivilly with a purposeful intent to harm their target.

8. Typology Of Deviant Workplace Behavior

Two Centers Of Deviant Workplace Behaviors

Researchers Robinson and Bennett (1995) examined workplace behaviors and proposed that there exist two centers of deviant workplace behavior. The two centers are identified around both the organizational focus and interpersonal focus.

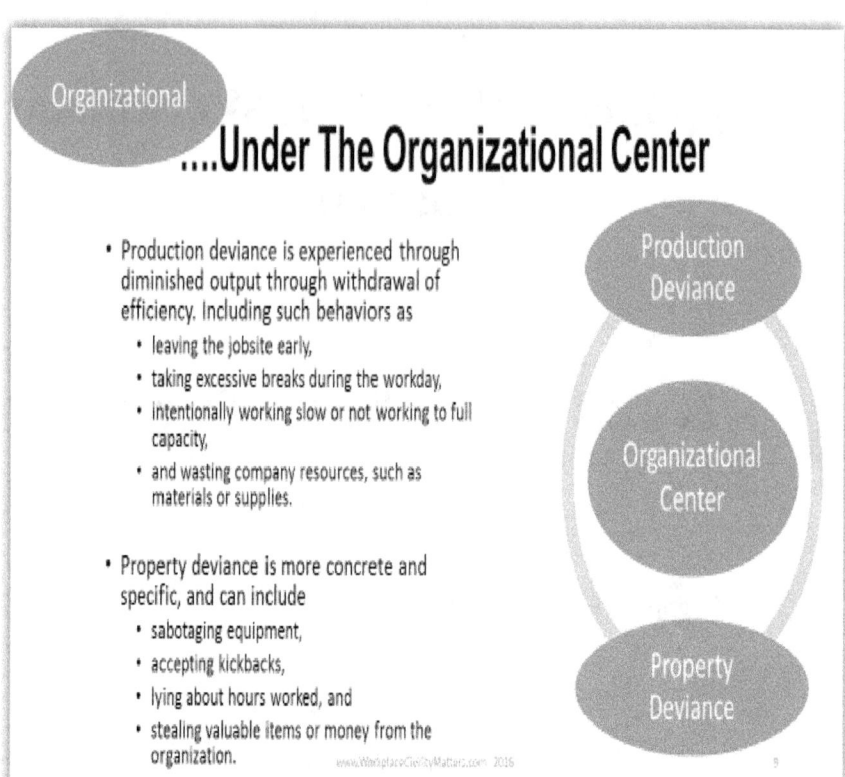

Understanding The Organizational Center

Under the organizational focus, the company or the workgroup could expect to observe either production or property deviance. Production deviance is experienced through diminished output by withdrawal of efficiency. Adverse production deviance typically encompasses such behaviors as leaving the jobsite early, taking excessive breaks during the workday, intentionally working slow or not working to full capacity, and wasting company resources, such as materials or supplies. In contrast, property deviance is more concrete and specific, and can include sabotaging equipment, accepting kickbacks, lying about hours worked, and stealing valuable items or money from the organization.

Understanding The Interpersonal Center

Under the interpersonal focus, the company or workgroup could expect to observe either political deviance or personal aggression. Political deviance disrupts the overall wellbeing of the organization, and typically encompasses such behaviors as signaling out individual employees for either harsh treatment or positive favoritism, gossiping about co-workers, blaming coworkers, and competing non-beneficially at the expense of colleagues within the workgroup. In contrast, personal aggression includes deviant interpersonal behaviors such as sexual harassment, emotional and verbal abuse, bullying or teasing, creating a threatening, antagonistic, or unpleasant working environment, stealing from co-workers, and purposely endangering coworkers.

The spectrum of deviant workplace behavior is broad, yet it is recognized along the continuum of behaviors that leads to the destruction of property, physical aggression, violence and even murder. As outlined earlier, acts of incivility are recognized as gateway behaviors that often escalate and cross over into violence.

9. Recognizing Acts Of Workplace Incivility

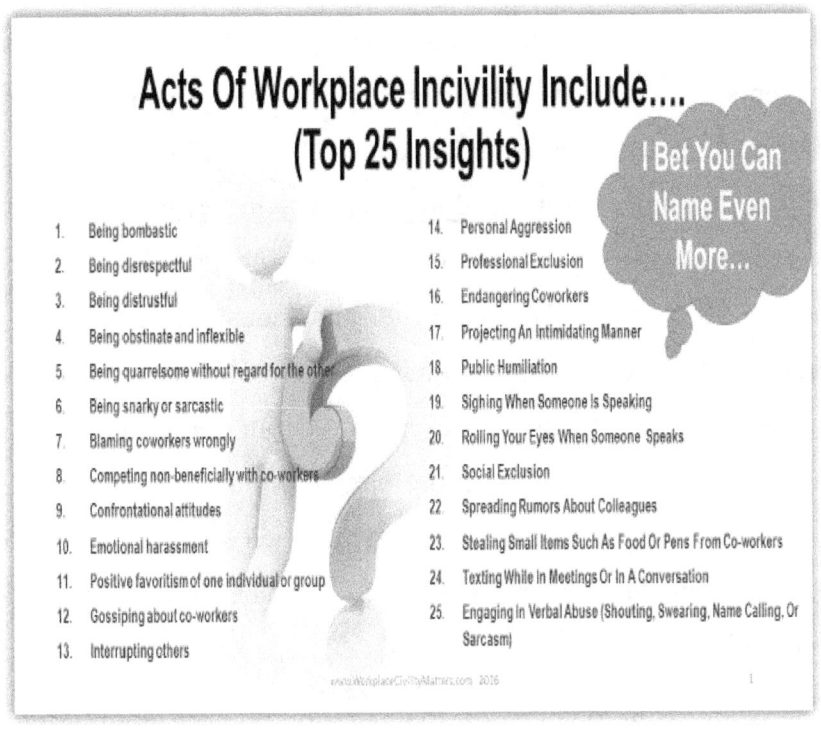

Twenty-Five Acts Of Incivility

Acts of incivility suck the happiness out of our workday. Bad behavior sucks! Disrespectful treatment of others sucks! Bullying sucks. Petty theft sucks. Emotional abuse sucks. Public shaming sucks. Professional humiliation sucks. Social isolation sucks. Quite simply workplace incivility sucks the happiness and joy out of our worklife.

Unfortunately, the prevalence of uncivil behaviors that occur within our society have escalated in recent years and have begun to spill over into our workplace. The internet and associated electronic connectivity and omnipresent technology have depersonalized our relationships. We e-mail, instant-message, and make anonymous comments in any number of forums. We endure a constant barrage of information and negative commentary. We react quickly, type and text with impunity, **and we don't censor ourselves**. We live in a time when anyone can type or text anything about anyone and have it read in all corners of the world instantaneously. It seems that the harshest comments are the ones that get the widest dissemination and the most attention. We shout our opinions from the rooftop or on the 24/7 news channels, and the more uncivil we are, the more airtime the media gives us. Pundits yelling at each another in political forums, or on the TV and the radio, have become a part of our everyday life.

As a consequence of the deterioration of civility within society in general, organizations must commit to tackling the issue and address these spillover behaviors within the workplace. The first step is to seek to understand and name the worklife nuisances that are the elements of workplace incivility. The following 25 insights are not intended to be an all-inclusive list; however they are intended to offer a perspective through which to explore and explain the phenomenon of workplace incivility.

#1. Workplace incivility includes being bombastic in your dealings with colleagues, subordinates, stakeholders, suppliers or customers.

#2. Workplace incivility includes being disrespectful in the event of disagreement with another. While disagreement is inevitable, it is unnecessary and unprofessional to make it personal or pugnacious.

#3. Workplace incivility includes being distrustful. As outlined in the opening section of this book, the prevalence of trust as a societal value is in decline. Being distrustful of fellow workers creates animosity and rancor. Distrust reflects an expectation that others' motives, intentions, actions, and behaviors are harmful to your interests, thereby creating a combative, rather than cooperative interaction.

#4. Workplace incivility includes being obstinate and inflexible in the face of organizational change or individual needs in regards to tactical performance, operational needs, or strategic direction.

#5. Workplace incivility includes being quarrelsome without regard for the wellbeing of another. A quarrelsome demeanor leads to interpersonal avoidance and organizational ambiguity in the absence of effective communication.

#6. Workplace incivility includes being snarky or sarcastic. Aggressive sarcasm that is designed intentionally to be belittling and hurtful undermines openness and creativity.

#7.Workplace incivility includes blaming coworkers wrongly and persistently for task failings or procedural errors.

#8.Workplace incivility includes competing non-beneficially with co-workers, and undermining their individual and group performance.

#9.Workplace incivility includes confrontational attitudes where combative interaction with other worklife practitioners disrupts effective communication and sharing of knowledge.

#10.Workplace incivility includes emotional harassment and causing emotional harm to others. Emotional harassment can include making rude gestures, repeated teasing, whispering about someone while in their presence, imitating someone's speech or behavior in a way designed to offend, or mockingly laughing at someone's mistakes.

#11.Workplace incivility includes positive favoritism of one individual or group at the expense of others.

#12.Workplace incivility includes gossiping about co-workers and contributing to adverse feelings towards other employees.

#13.Workplace incivility includes interrupting others when speaking, without allowing them to make their point or offer an alternative perspective.

#14.Workplace incivility includes personal aggression directed at other colleagues or subordinates.

#15.Workplace incivility includes professional exclusion. Professional exclusion of individuals or groups from meetings, networking opportunities, discussions or decisions, undermines the credibility and influence of those affected and signals to others in the workgroup their lack of relevance to the organization.

#16. Workplace incivility includes professionally or personally endangering coworkers. Endangerment of others in the workplace includes professional ridicule or personal taunting with the intent to cause damage to professional reputation or harm to personal or emotional wellbeing.

#17. Workplace incivility includes projecting an intimidating manner. Intimidation includes disrespecting others personal space, leaning in or getting in their face when speaking to them, holding eye contact or glaring at them. Other aspects of intimidation include standing over another while communicating, blocking egress through doorways, poking them in the chest while talking, widely gesticulating or raising your fist or hand as if to strike, or entrapping someone in a confined space such as a cubicle.

#18. Workplace incivility includes public humiliation. Shaming a colleague or subordinate for performance errors, berating or chastising them in front of others, sarcastically questioning their judgment or thinking processes, causing them to be embarrassed unnecessarily in front of parties unrelated to the discussion or issue at hand.

#19. Workplace incivility includes purposely sighing when someone is speaking. By making disinterested or annoyed sounds or vocalizations, and loudly sighing with contempt, for the purpose of embarrassing or humiliating another diminishes their credibility in front of others, and attack their confidence and undermines their competence.

#20.Workplace incivility includes rolling your eyes when someone speaks. By rolling your eyes with contempt, you are signaling a lack of regard for their wellbeing or professional contribution, which serves to diminish their confidence in their professional competence.

#21.Workplace incivility includes social exclusion. Social exclusion of individuals or groups from coffee chats, lunches, after-work gatherings or work-related sporting activities undermines the group dynamic and sense of belonging, and signals to others their lack of relevance to the workgroup.

#22.Workplace incivility includes spreading rumors about colleagues. The groundless chatter when a colleague is *"called upstairs"*. The emails back and forth guessing which work unit will suffer the largest budget cuts, or hasn't met performance expectations. This type of interaction is harmful and costly. It wastes time, damages reputations, promotes divisiveness, creates anxiety, and destroys morale.

#23.Workplace incivility includes stealing small items such as food or pens from co-workers. Taking candy from your colleagues' candy dish when they are absent, of their slice of cake from the office refrigerator, or pens or supplies from their desk, may seem either humorous or just a small nuisance behavior. However, it represents a disregard for their personal property or work resources, and signals disrespect.

#24.Workplace incivility includes texting while in meetings or engaged in a conversation. None of us like to be slighted or ignored when we are speaking. Omnipresent personal electronic devices have enhanced our connectedness in the workplace. However, they have also led to a new domain for acts of incivility. Which, if you want to damage further your work relationships, will provide ample opportunity through their ease of use, and almost hypnotic usurpation of our attention.

#25.Workplace incivility includes engaging in verbal abuse (shouting, swearing, name calling, or sarcasm) as opposed to effective communication. Verbal abuse in the workplace is intended to be intimidating, offensive, demeaning, or to belittle another person or group.

10. Who Are The Players In Incivility?

The Players In Incivility

While business outcomes and organizational performance are quantifiably impacted by workplace incivility, there are three discrete individual actors that play a role in workplace incivility. The three discrete participants in the workplace incivility paradigm are the instigator or perpetrator, the target, and the observer. The observer of workplace incivility is as equally significant as the target, as he is is adversely impacted in ways that the target is not, even when he is not part of the instigator-target dyad.

The role of each participant and their response to acts of incivility varies depending upon either the individual involved or the context of the behavior. What may appear as direct and specific deviant behavior to one party can be interpreted as a minor nuisance to another? As an executive coach to individuals who may experience pushback from colleagues or subordinates as a result of their deviant workplace behavior, we often hear their rationalization that the "complainers" are too thin-skinned, and just need to toughen up! As an executive coach, we help such clients to explore an alternative perspective, which is to take their workplace complainers as they find them, rather than expecting others to change to accommodate their needs and behaviors. This perspective is especially true when dealing with subordinates and other stakeholders where influence rather than threats are the force behind getting things done.

The Instigator

Who is that guy? Who is the instigator? The instigator of incivility is generally someone in a position of power over another, either organizationally, or socially, or though influence, and who behaves uncivilly in order to either assert or preserve his power.

Instances may occur where the instigator inadvertently damages the target by some innocuous behavior, and is unaware of the effect or the outcome. However, the ability for instigators to obfuscate purposeful acts of incivility and masquerade them as innocent or socially inept transgressions is powerful and insidious.

The nature of the uncivil behaviors only sometimes expose the intentionality of the resolve to harm. Research suggests that instigators of workplace incivility do not differentiate because of gender or age, although typically the effort is aimed at individuals with less positional power. The instigator of workplace incivility can be anyone, although twice as many people surveyed admitted to being a target as opposed to an instigator of workplace incivility.

The Target

Employees subjected to workplace incivility are referred to as targets. Targets are not merely thin-skinned employees who are easily offended or who perceive a personal slight in every interaction. However, as a consequence of having endured workplace incivility the targets of deviant behavior become more sensitive to, and are sensitized by the existence of the phenomenon. Among targets of workplace incivility, their views of organizational injustice and professional ostracism differ, depending upon both their organizational status and the status of the instigator. The research of Milam, Spitzmueller, and Penney (2009) focused on discrete differences within the "...*big Five Personality Traits...*"

among targets of workplace incivility. The Big Five personality traits is a widely explored theory of five broad dimensions used by psychologists to explain human personality and consciousness. The five factors have been identified as openness to experience, conscientiousness, extraversion, agreeableness, and neuroticism. Milam et al. suggested a "...*negative relation between agreeableness and incivility, a positive relation between neuroticism and incivility, and a negative relation between extraversion and incivility...*"

The discoveries of various researchers suggest that certain traits exhibited by targets, including disagreeableness, neuroticism and introversion, are significant with regards to opening them up to acts of incivility, or exacerbating the impact of the behaviors upon their person. Research suggests that of all the traits considered, a low level of agreeableness among targets incited more frequent occurrence of acts of workplace incivility than high agreeableness. When this insight is discussed among workgroups certain coworkers confirmed that disagreeable individuals typically invited more uncivil behavior than did their more agreeable colleagues.

Employees who exhibited high neuroticism perceived incivility more negatively, and the neurotic employee can be categorized by traits such as excessive worrying, nervousness, insecurity, or self-pity; such that certain workplace occurrences that may seem inoffensive to less neurotic observers may be perceived by them as acts incivility. In our worklife we often jokingly commented that '*you don't have to be a psychiatrist to work here but if you are it helps*.' The truth behind this tongue-in-cheek humor is that as managers we do well to be more cognizant of how an employee's personality traits affect job performance, which in turn helps us to understand their perception of and response to workplace incivility. Notwithstanding the hazard of attempting to turn our managers into amateur psychologists, interpersonal understanding of the complexities of the human dynamic helps establish the framework and language for a constructive work environment; especially when we consider the value proposition offered by the new employee, which is affect rather than effect.

The Observer

Workplace incivility spillover occurs when observers are negatively affected by the deviant behaviors of the instigator-target dyad. Surprise and anger are the two most common responses experienced by observers in response to incivility, although researchers differ on the degree of impact. While one perspective suggests that observers are not as significantly impacted by incivility as are the targets, another perspective suggests that they are more deeply impacted by vicarious exposure to mistreatment. They are impacted by feelings of powerlessness, which takes a substantial toll on employee wellbeing. Specifically observers of incivility are psychologically affected by the perceived injustice and unfairness of the interaction, and can experience a deep sense of shame for not being able to intercede or prevent the incident. As a side note our coaching experience affirms that often the observer in the incivility triad is sometimes more deeply impacted than the nature of the incident would otherwise suggest. Observer or bystander guilt seems to be motivated by a feeling of failure to act or support for the target.

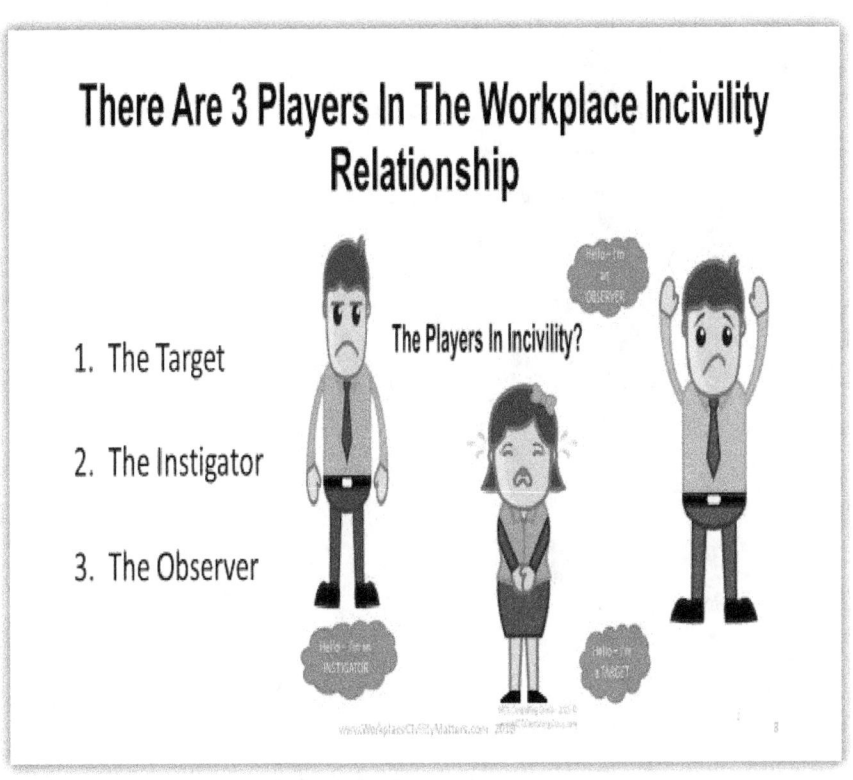

Naming The Players In Incivility

11. The Ambiguity Of Incivility

The Ambiguity Of Incivility

Prevailing research and associated theories about the phenomenon of workplace incivility, as well as our experience as a leadership practitioners and executive coaches have shaped our insight into the individual and organizational impact of deviant workplace behaviors. Workplace incivility is defined by Andersson & Pearson as *"...low-intensity deviant behavior with ambiguous intent to harm the target, in violation of workplace norms for mutual respect"*. Cortina (2008) built upon the earlier premise of ambiguity and proposed that incivility is *"...a veiled manifestation of sexism and racism in organizations..."*.

From a coaching perspective, we have come to understand that selective incidences of incivility can be a contrivance or subterfuge through which racial, and gender inequalities persevere within organizations. We have inferred from a variety of comments made by several coaching clients that certain rude or uncivil behaviors, which they have personally experienced, resembled a veiled manifestation of sexism or racism. It has become clear that the ambiguous nature of incivility can easily obfuscate the instigators true harmful intent; notwithstanding an organizations' rigorous prevention and training programs, which are designed to eliminate conscious biases, sexism and racism in the workplace. Awareness of the possibility that such an old nuisance is being hidden as ambiguous workplace incivility may help underscore for leaders, managers, and influencers the need to vigorously respond to all deviant workplace behaviors, including incivility.

We have observed that within a dysfunctional workplace negligent antidiscrimination policies, permissive leadership behaviors, and the occurrence of antisocial behaviors emboldens employees to act upon their biases. Traditional patterns of deviant behavior such as cultural bias, racism, and sexism can re-emerge as vague incivilities disguised as rude behavior. The ambiguous nature of workplace incivility obfuscates the possible intended and covert discrimination of such actions.

The distinctive ambiguity of intent to harm isolates workplace incivility from other forms of deviant behavior within organizations. The ambiguity of intent appears to impede awareness of the phenomenon of workplace incivility, and without awareness or understanding your organizations' leaders, managers, and influencers have little incentive to explore factors that deter incivility or encourage civility within the work environment.

Even within a healthy and inclusive organization the ambiguous characteristic of workplace incivility offers an avenue for hostile instigators to perpetuate malfeasance, often just below the radar of an otherwise watchful organization's traditional response mechanism. The significance of this point cannot be overstated; that the vagueness component of incivility, that is the inherent ambiguity, is part of what makes the phenomenon so insidious.

As worklife participants and as executive coaches we have observed that many individual acts of incivility are not bad enough to invoke adverse management actions. Leaders, managers, and influencers are frequently unaware of the phenomenon or its effect on personnel and performance because of the inherent ambiguity of workplace incivility. Unaware leaders, managers and influencers who do not recognize either the antecedents or the organizational effects of workplace incivility, usually do so to the detriment of targets and observers; as well as at a cost to performance outcomes for their organization.

12. The Cost To Workers And Workplaces

Incivility And The Cost To Workers And The Workplace

Incivility and poor workplace behavior has many faces. However, the results are usually the same. Business outcomes and organizational performance are diminished when employees are distracted by deviant workplace behaviors. The new affect employee is significantly more impacted by deviant behavior than his recent predecessor, the knowledge worker.

This is a simple truth as his individual feelings and affect are an integral part of the contemporary organizations' performance outcome equation. Today's effective employee is valued more for his affect than his knowledge, (hence, he is referred to as an affect worker). As a consequence of his relationship to the organizations' performance outcome his ongoing wellbeing is critical to the businesses' wellbeing. Interpersonal affect travels faster than the speed of light, and a negatively affected employee can rapidly create adverse performance spirals throughout your organization.

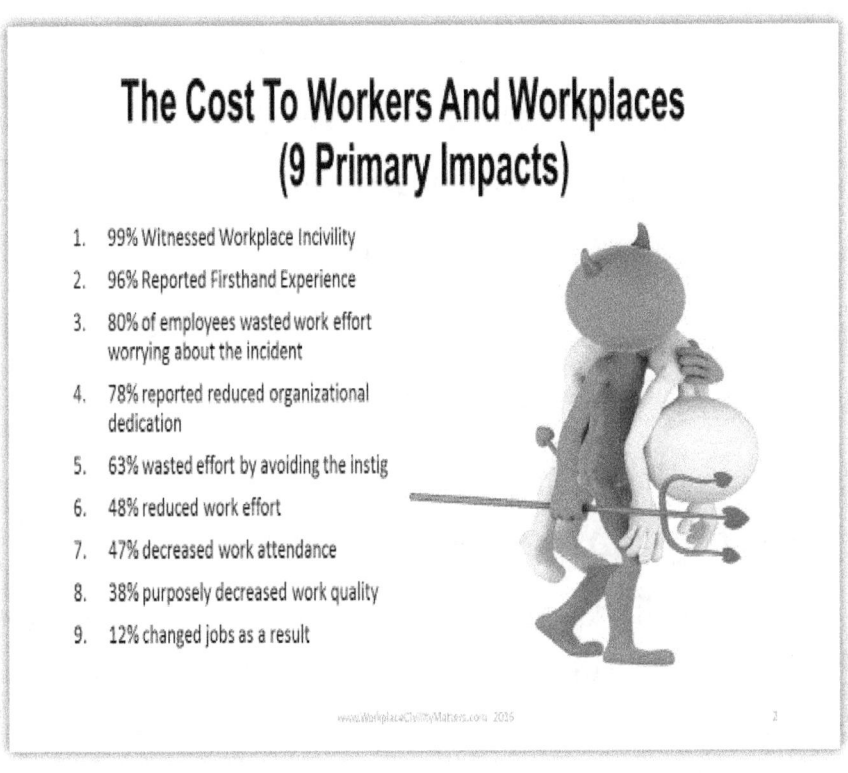

The Cost To Workers And Workplaces

Significantly however, and notwithstanding the link between employee wellbeing and employee affect, data about the prevalence of workplace incivility is significant. Among thousands of employees surveyed across various industries and job levels research shows that the prevalence and impact of workplace incivility is staggering;

> ➢ 99% witnessed workplace incivility
>
> ➢ 96% reported firsthand experience
>
> ➢ 80% of wasted work effort worrying about the incident
>
> ➢ 78% reported reduced organizational dedication
>
> ➢ 63% wasted effort by avoiding the instigator
>
> ➢ 48% reduced work effort
>
> ➢ 47% decreased work attendance
>
> ➢ 38% purposely decreased work quality
>
> ➢ 12% changed jobs

99% Witnessed Workplace Incivility

As we now know, acts of incivility can be the precursor to acts of violence. Earlier sections of this book addressed statistics reported by the U.S. government about the million-plus acts of violence in the workplace each year. It is a shocking statement about the condition of our contemporary work lives, yet who was counting or measuring the numerous acts of incivility which led up to these acts of violence.

96% Reported Firsthand Experience

More than nine of every ten employees surveyed reported firsthand experience with workplace incivility. In a work culture where employee affect is the new value proposition, how effective can these employees be if they are exposed to deviant workplace behaviors while in the performance of their organizational role?

80% Of Employees Wasted Work Effort Worrying About The Incident.

If more than nine of every ten employees surveyed reported firsthand experience with workplace incivility, and 80% of those are wasting work effort worrying about the incident, it is safe to say that seven of every ten employees are not focused on their job at some point during their worklife. This would translate to seven of every ten employees not fully meeting the expectations of their value proposition, and not fully contributing to your organizations' bottom line.

78% Reported Reduced Organizational Dedication

Withholding one's discretionary contribution is the difference between giving the organization simply what they pay you for and giving them your best and most creative and affective self. Almost eight out of ten employees are withholding their highest and best self from their organization as a result of the presence of uncivil behaviors in their workplace.

63% Wasted Effort By Avoiding The Instigator

Taking the long way back from the bathroom, or circumnavigating the cubicle farm in order to sidestep one's instigator is a logical response and an effective way to ward off other acts of incivility. The downside is that time spent purposely avoiding one's nemesis is also time lost from production, communication, creation, and positively affecting other employees and performance outcomes.

48% Reduced Work Effort

Working slow in response to incidents of workplace incivility reflects a conscious effort to harm the organization, as opposed to getting back at the target. This is a well-documented and easily understood phenomenon that employees will strike back at the organization rather than their tormentor in an attempt to balance out their sense of unfairness or injustice. Almost five out of every ten employees are reducing their work effort by engaging in their own personal tantrum, and do so just below the radar of the organizational efficiency eagles. Their reduced work effort is sufficiently benign that it won't get them into trouble, yet the cumulative effect on performance outcomes can have a substantial impact upon your organization.

47% Decreased Work Attendance

Calling in well as opposed to calling in sick is the preferred punitive response for almost half of all employees who have experienced workplace incivility. These are employees who otherwise have had a positive attitude about their work, and their attendance is reflective of their organizational commitment. Absenteeism, which can be defined as either intentional or habitual absence from work, is counterproductive for the organization as it results in decreased productivity and performance outcomes.

38% Purposely Decreased Work Quality

Almost four in every ten employees will purposely extract revenge from the organization by exercising the age-old tactic of reducing work quality or work product sabotage. Decreased work quality underscores the relationship between perceived injustice and workplace incivility, and can harm the organizations reputation, especially when as poor quality product enters the market place creating dissatisfied customers and consumers.

12% Changed Jobs As A Result

Over one in every ten employees will change jobs as a result of experiencing or observing workplace incivility. High employee turnover can have an adverse impact on performance goals and business outcomes, as well as on the emotional state of fellow employees. Also significance is the timing of the impacted employees' departure from your organization. From amongst those employees who leave, the reason is ambiguous as targets do not always reveal the reason for leaving, yet they take time in planning their exit strategy and are purposefully underproductive in the weeks and months leading up to their departure.

The Price Is Right

Although this section of the book is intended to address the price or cost or harm of incivility to an organization we have merely scratched the surface of the damage it causes. We have not asked the instigator about his awareness of the impact of his behaviors on the organizations bottom-line, nor his regard for business outcomes and productivity.

What we do know however that half of all managers interviewed presented an awareness of having experienced being an instigator of workplace incivility. In most instances however, their description or recollection of the event was benign, suggesting a purposeful detachment or diminishing of the significance or severity of their behavior. The six million dollar question is that if acts of incivility are so prevalent, how is it that so few are unaware that their behavior is uncivil. Awareness of and a conscious effort to quantify the linkage between deviant behaviors and performance outcomes is critical towards mitigating the prevalence and impact of workplace incivility in your organization.

Part Two: 40 Keys To Civility

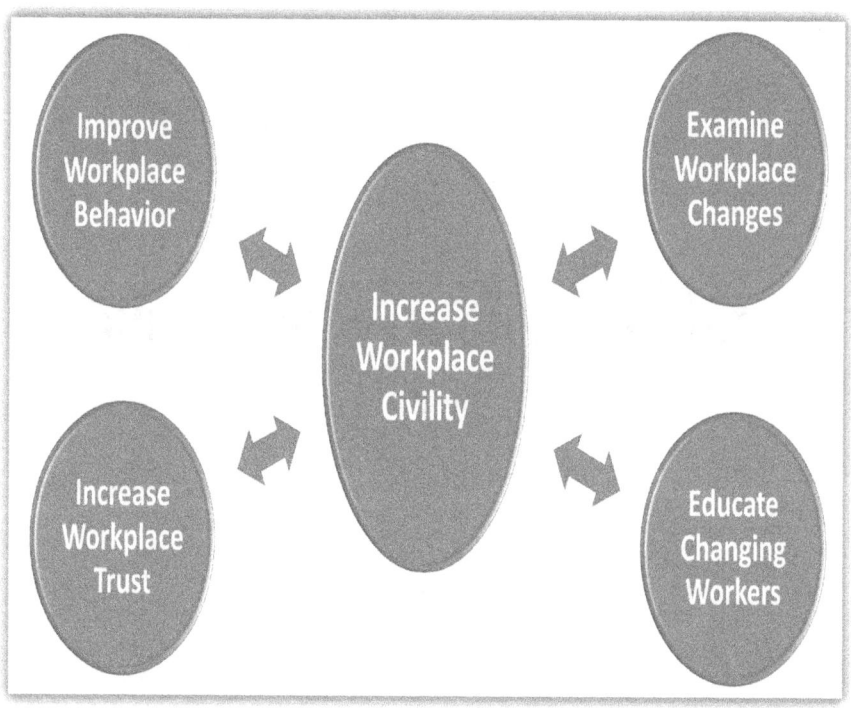

Chapter 13

13. The Antithesis Of Workplace Incivility

Workplace Civility (The Antithesis Of Workplace Incivility)

Part two of this book is designed to address the *'now what'* of workplace incivility. The first part of the book gave a name to the contemporary phenomenon of deviant workplace behavior and an explanation of how we have arrived at this point. Workplace incivility occurs as a result of four distinct social and workplace changes. These are the (1) external influences of the rise of deviant social behavior, (2) the decline in societal and familial trust, (3) the changes in the contemporary workplace, and (4) the evolving and changing distinctions of the contemporary or knowledge worker, who more recently has become known as the affect worker. The next paragraphs offer forty strategies and tactics that you as a manager, leader or influencer can begin to employ today towards creating and sustaining a civil workplace.

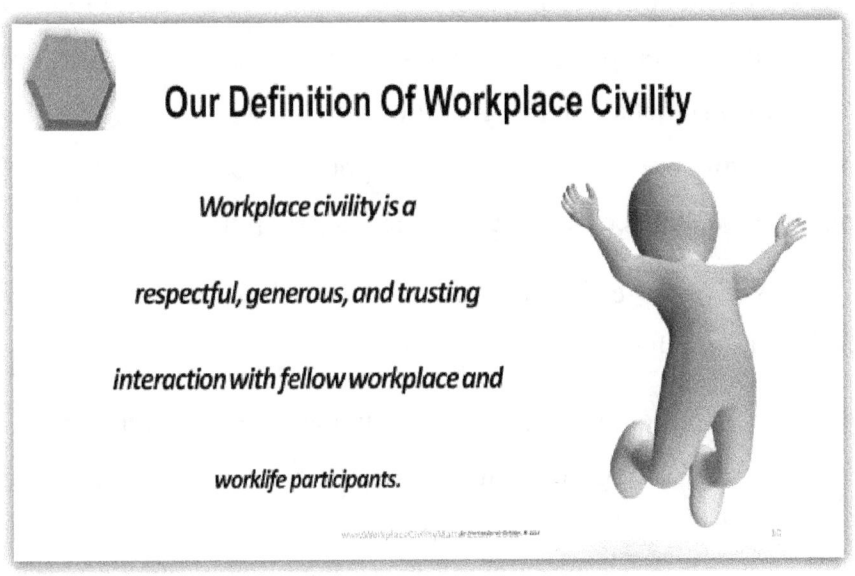

Our Definition Of Civility

Not all of the forty improvement strategies are necessary for every individual or every organization. Rather they are offered for consideration after you have completed an assessment and analysis of your organizations' level of workplace incivility, and decided on the focus areas you wish to pursue.

Before going any further however we want to offer a frame of reference for what a civil organization can be. We begin by recognizing that workplace civility is the opposite of the confrontational attitudes and deviant behaviors, intimidating manners, and rudeness that encompasses workplace incivility. The graphic above, which represents the interactive link between a positive or civil workplace culture, trust building, educating employees about the impact of deviant social behaviors, and examining workplace changes and associated declining organizational behaviors. The goal of the following forty strategies is to offer you the tools from which you can begin to reverse the impact of workplace incivility and develop a civil workplace.

We propose the definition of Workplace Civility is built on three distinct pillars:

- ✓ Being respectful, even in the face of disagreement
- ✓ Being generous, even where there is a cost to doing so
- ✓ Being trusting, even when there is a risk to being so

Workplace civility is a respectful, generous, and trusting interaction with fellow workplace and worklife participants.

Workplace Civility is a <u>Respectful</u>, <u>Generous</u>, and <u>Trusting</u> interaction with fellow workplace and worklife participants.

Being Respectful | Being Generous | Being Trusting

Even In The Face Of Disagreement | Even Where There Is A Cost To Doing So | Even When There Is A Risk To Being So

The Three Pillars Of Civility

The question that remains is whether worklife practitioners, leaders, managers, and influencers have the knowledge, skills and ability to positively affect the behaviors of others against an onslaught of deviant behaviors within the contemporary workplace? We know that negative workplace interactions are linked to negative outcomes, such as reduced engagement or retaliation. Therefore, any proposal for identifying, developing, and mastering positive workplace interactions is intended to boost and improve work-related outcomes.

14. The 40 Keys

Key #1: Applaud Civil Behavior. The problem is that more often than not we pour our intellectual and emotional energy into confronting or addressing or mitigating uncivil behavior in the workplace. We do this at the expense of affirming or acknowledging civil behavior. We focus our efforts and energy on the deviant behaviors of the instigator and his impact on the organization. The contamination pathways through the organization, along which acts of incivility travel, are also the same pathways that acts of civility can travel to positively affect the workplace. Why not consider refocusing some of our energy?

An unconventional workplace culture improvement strategy would be to go out of your way to observe, recognize, and applaud civil behaviors in others, which by default will energize the incivility detoxification process. Use the act of acknowledgment to stimulate preferred workplace behaviors that support a civil environment.

Practice the behavior of 'catching someone in the act of civility' and then call them on their behavior. We recognize that some might believe that exuberant support, praise, and encouragement are often considered insincere or calculating. In fact, we also recognize that a focused and public effort to applaud civil behavior in others may appear to be a contrivance or an overkill; however we are aware that in the game of effective leadership followers will follow their leaders lead! Remember the old management thought processes that use to reverberate through the C-Suite that went something like this "...*If you can't measure it, you can't manage it...*"? Well from a workplace civility perspective, the vast majority of significant worklife issues that we need to manage aren't measurable; from the interpersonal competence of new recruits, to the confidence we instill in a new supervisor, to the executive presence we imbue in an emerging manager. The contemporary management perspective is that we manage these unmeasurable states of leadership behavior perfectly well without any need for metrics. We manage these states by example, and what leaders and influencers do matters to the culture of your organization. Because we manage these states by actively demonstrating, imbuing, and focusing on preferred behaviors, others will follow your lead. And Why? Because someone is always watching.

The behaviors we exemplify, focus on, and amplify through our acts of civility are the behaviors we can improve in others. You can reinforce the organizational value of engaging civility towards others by publicly acknowledging such positive behaviors. Applauding civil behaviors should be done publicly and should be specific, meaningful, accurate, relevant and timely to when the incident of civility occurred. Consider the following "Applaud Civil Behavior" Leadership Examples:

➢Team, I want to acknowledge Joe, as I appreciate his quickly bringing the group back on task during our staff meeting.

➢During our heated staff meeting this morning we made some great progress on the issue of the reorganization, and I just want to acknowledge all of you for your civility, and your willingness to do this difficult work together in such a professional manner.

➢Thanks for sharing that insight with the group Jane. It is a controversial issue and it took a lot of courage for you to do that.

➢Thank you John for taking responsibility for the delay in delivering the final reports and not blaming others.

➢Bill, thanks for volunteering to take notes on the whiteboard today, as it helped to keep us focused and I really appreciate it.

➢Jill, thanks for sharing your frustrations with the group in such a professional way and not making it personal. We can all better understand the impact of the delay on your unit's schedule

Key #2: Be A Coach. The problem is that more often than not we as leaders and managers succumb to being directive as opposed to being co-creative. This happens especially when we are under pressure to produce results or during a crisis. The manager-as-coach leadership philosophy requires a shift in management practices from over-reliance on the traditional top-down, directive and hierarchical approach.

The manager-as-coach philosophy encourages and emboldens the affect worker to bring forth his creativity, which generates bottom-up ideas and adds value to the organization. A primary role of leadership is to create new leaders, by encouraging effective communications and helping others to co-create positive performance outcomes. Leaders unleash their followers potential by imparting trust through authenticity, clarity of purpose, and openness to personal growth through continual learning. Become the coach to your workgroup.

Key #3: Be Consistent. The problem is that when we are not consistent, we give mixed messages to our followers, and undermine others confidence in our leadership. You have experienced this for yourself no doubt, sitting in the board/staff/team meeting room, only to be stunned by the attitude, manner and message from your leader who, just days earlier espoused a completely different position or perspective. One day your leader is measured and reserved in his push for continuous improvements. The next day, the same leader has donned the mantle of Genghis Khan, demeaning the team and threatening their careers. When asked (by brave mortals) about his fluctuating behaviors and tactics, the leader declares that he '*believes in situational leadership.*' Situational leadership never deserved such a bad name!

What he is really saying is that he offers a poor excuse for leadership behaviors that include inconsistency and unpredictability. Inconsistent leadership can be the death of a team... although being a consistent jerk can be really bad for team health. By way of example, when you, as a leader present your values and priorities you should be consistent by complying with them yourself. You should not, for example, represent yourself as that boss who respects employees' boundaries and personal time; and then text, e-mail and call them during non-work hours and expect immediate response to non-critical issues.

Key #4: Be Courteous. The problem is that sometimes we are so overwhelmed by the events going on around us that we forget to be our highest and best selves. Yes, we forget to be courteous. Leaders distinguish themselves by their courteous behavior. In the workplace courteous behavior assures access to and influence among likeminded professionals.

Did you know however, that the art of courtesy has a very old and elegant history? In 1528, the Italian courtier, diplomat, and renaissance author Baldisseri Castiglione, penned an instructional guide titled *The Book of the Courtier*. The content of Castiglione's book served as a courtesy manual for aspiring young gentlemen and addressed contemporary issues of etiquette and morality for the aspiring courtier. The book became influential in 16th-century European circles as young men of commerce aspired to have greater influence in society by emulating the courteous behaviors of highborn individuals. Even before Castiglione penned his book, the culture of courtesy had begun to spread among the elite of the emerging nation states within Europe. Without social refinement and knowledge of being courteous, you would have been excluded from such influential opportunities. Why? Because the knowledge of courteous behaviors offered access to power and social status.

Reading the classics was also prevalent, as it was designed to have a moral effect and produce a balanced and virtuous character. However, Castiglione's Book of the Courtier was more pragmatic as it instructed young men in civilized deportment and social living, such as forgoing antisocial behaviors which include public belching, spitting, and eating with their hands.

The lesson for today is that when a leader forgets or forgoes courteous behavior, their access and influence is diminished as they are not perceived as being a part of the educated inner circle. Be courteous, least others think you are not a member of their group.

Key #5: Be Kind. The problem is that sometimes we are so exhausted from work and miserable in ourselves that we forget our most basic duty – which is to be kind! Be kind, for everyone you meet is fighting a harder battle. Be kind because it is reasonable to assume that on this journey through life that we all must travel there are fellow travelers on our road that are also fighting a hard battle. Whether their obstacles are greater, their resources fewer, or their temptations fiercer, they too have doubts and fears, perhaps they endure unhappy memories and wounds from their past battles that are only barely healed, so take the time to be kind.

It cannot be overstated here that we all endure many challenges in our life and some of us come through them less well than others. When we remember that we are all human beings traveling the same road on our life journey we are able to engage more kindly with our fellow traveler, and therefore we can choose to wish him well on his journey. We do not have to pile on the misery or add additional obstacles when we can choose to be kind to another human being.

Key #6: Be The Blues Brothers. The problem is that we don't always start our plans and projects with the end in sight. Workplace incivility festers in an environment where the mission is unclear, or when it is not clearly communicated to the workgroup. The iconic 1980's Blues Brothers movie is both instructional as a management parable, and as a comedic tale of redemption for Jake Blues and his brother Elwood. As the plot unfolds the two brothers undertake "*a mission from God*" to save from foreclosure the orphanage where they grew up. The Blues Brothers had 11 days to earn $5,000 to pay the property tax bill to the Cook County assessor's office. So they decide to reunite their Rhythm and Blues band and organize a concert to earn the money. While undertaking their mission, they were beleaguered by a psychopathic "mystery woman", rabid Neo-Nazis, and a violent Country and Western band, all-the-while being pursued by officers of the law. If Jake and

Elwood sat down and penned their management strategy it was probably lost to the cutting room floor. However, at a minimum, a management strategy answers four basic questions about the project; Why? What? Who? And When? To avoid creating uncertainty and spawning acts of incivility in your workgroup can you answer and communicate to your team the following questions? Why? - Why is the project being sponsored, or why is it necessary, or what is the compelling reason to execute? What? - What is the work that must be performed to make the project successful? What are the intermittent steps? What are the major products/deliverables? Who? - Who will be involved in the execution, and what is their role within the project? How will they be organized? When? - When is the work product due or when is the projects' drop dead date? For the Blues Brothers, their mission was clear. They were intent on raising $5000 to pay a tax bill, by bringing their band back together and holding a concert within 11 days. They were *"on a mission from God."*

Key #7: Conduct "Behavior Reviews" (versus Performance Reviews). The problem is that we are well versed in conducting performance reviews as they relate to the organizations' strategy. However, it's very seldom we ever conduct an effective behavior review, because we don't see the link to desired outcomes. Deviant employee behaviors that we put up with become the organizational behaviors we end up with and they impact performance outcomes.

An unconventional workplace improvement strategy would be to build into the employees' feedback mechanism a recurring behavior review, which would be conducted separately from the performance review process. The significance of conducting employee behavior reviews is that over time we have come to understand that employee behavior is as equally important as employee performance in relation to achieving the organization's goals and objectives. A high performing employee whose behavior is suboptimum or toxic can do more harm to the performance potential of others, and to the organization, than the cumulative value of his high-performance outcomes. The underlying premise for conducting behavior reviews is that the organizations' strategic objectives are achieved through individuals and through their behavior towards and with the organization. Therefore, conducting a behavior review provides an opportunity to assess and provide feedback on how each employee's behavior is aligned with your organization's culture, norms and strategic goals. If the employee's organizational behavior is counterproductive then the long-term value of their performance outcome is diminished.

Key #8: Build Trust. The problem is that we have come of age in a society where trust is in limited supply, and this lack of interpersonal trust has seeped into the workplace. Trust within organizational life is complex, simply because the workplace is made up of individuals with varying capacity for and degrees of trust in each other and for their organization. Even when you hire individuals with demonstrable personal integrity, the journey toward building a trusting and trustworthy organization is difficult. Research points to the link between trust and performance outcomes, and we know that lack of trust gives rise to acts of incivility. Conversely the presence of incivility is often a symptom of a distrustful organization.

When employees trust their colleagues and their leaders, they are more inclined to constructively resolve disagreements. Employees will be more creative, take risks, work harder, and contribute more of their discretionary value to the organization and other employees. When they don't trust their colleagues and leaders, employees will disengage and withhold their creativity and discretionary contribution. How then is trust built? Well, the components of trust building can be found in an effective manager's toolkit, although they have to be applied with rigor. Trust stems from or is diluted by basic leadership behaviors such as constancy, professional competence, consistency, emotional contagion, clear communication, and the courage to confront and resolve difficult issues. Committing to build or sustain organizational trust requires an offensive strategy and it begins with being aware of how your actions and behaviors measure up against this list. Building trust also requires a defensive strategy, which includes vigorously addressing the above behaviors in yourself and others that can dilute organizational trust. Perceived lapses in constancy and loyalty towards each employee creates a sense of injustice and require a focused response. If damaged trust left unattended the results will fester and eat away at the heart and soul of the organization and contribute to new incivility spirals reaching far beyond the initial location of the damage.

Professional competence builds trust, and incompetence dilutes trust. If skills are lacking then making training available will help the situation, but if the individual is incapable of performing the job no amount of training will improve the situation. This is where the courage to confront difficult personnel decisions is critical to building trust. Consistency in behavior, managing your emotional self, addressing the emotional outbursts of others, and clearly communicating expectations also serve as the foundation for building more trust.

Key #9: Check The Climate. The problem is that oftentimes we are so focused on performance outcomes and the bottom line that we fail to remain aware of the climate, culture or health of the organization. A positive organizational climate in the workplace not only helps to keep our employees more motivated, but research also suggests they are more creative and engaged; which results in higher performance outcomes and a healthier bottom-line. Workplace incivility eats away at a positive organizational climate.

Civil leaders can make the greatest difference in their workplace climate, and uncivil leaders destroy a positive climate. So helping them to understand the climate they create is a key step in improving organizational performance. Either through a formal climate or culture survey, or an informal assessment of indicators such as the loci or source of complaints, grievances, or absenteeism, you can assess both the climate and your leaders' impact on their workgroup's motivation and ability to execute. By assessing general and local climate of your organization, you can help leaders gain insight to how their actions drive team results. You can then set the stage for leadership improvement through one-to-one feedback and group development workshops.

Key #10: Check Yourself. The problem is that we are merely human, and as busy humans we don't always take time out to reflect on our behaviors. We tend to lose a sense of ourselves through a lack of self-awareness. A leader's attitude is contagious and is caught by his followers more rapidly that his actions, so check yourself. How does your attitude betray you? Is your professed attitude about civilized behaviors and workplace civility incongruent with your words and actions? Employees learn to be civil and ethical in part by observing leaders who stand up for doing what is right, especially when the leader is successful as a result of his positive actions.

As a leader your attitude is influential, as is your power to influence others because you make decisions about the rewards and punishments imposed on them as employees. Your followers learn about acceptable behavior by observing what happens to others. Are you aware how your attitude and your behavior is perceived by your workgroup?

Key #11: Commit To A Higher Purpose. The problem is that we aspire to make changes in our life, or to make a difference in the lives of others; however we never actually make a commitment or follow through with the plan. How many times have you abandoned your New Year's resolutions after one week? Or after two, four or six months? Well, we know that most New Year's resolutions don't work. But surprisingly setting and writing down your goals does. Research shows that you are substantially more likely to achieve your goals just by writing them down. If you aspire to create a civil workplace you will be more successful when you write down your specific goal.

Writing your goals down is important for several reasons. It will force you to clarify what you truly want regarding a civil workplace and it will motivate you to take action concerning your own behavior. It will serve as a sorting mechanism for other civility enhancing possibilities, and it will help you to overcome the resistance brought about by believing the task of creating a civil workplace is just too hard. Having a written statement, albeit an aspirational one, will help you to see and rejoice in each small victory towards achieving your goal.

Key #12: Communicate Effectively. The problem is when we don't know how to communicate effectively we will miscommunicate, which leaves room for ambiguity, distrust, and uncivil responses in the face of uncertainty. Communication can be any exchange of information between the sender and receiver. The sender is the person communicating the message, while the receiver is the person interpreting the message. This process, known as the traditional sender-receiver model, is affected by how we each use our five senses; seeing, hearing, touch, taste, and smell, to interpret our world. Other factors, such as life experience, education, and knowledge also contribute to how we receive information.

Culture also affects the communication process in the way that we send and interpret messages. Intercultural communication can add significant complexity to the communication process and create greater ambiguity, misunderstanding and possible offense. As if intercultural communications was not challenging enough, communication between people of the same culture can also cause challenges because of different types of communication styles, ranging from assertive to aggressive to expressive. Are you communicating effectively?

Key #13: Count To Ten. The problem is that in the face of a threat we allow our higher functioning or logical brain to become hijacked by our emotional brain. When faced with a threatening situation our emotional response can take over the rest of our brain in the blink of an eye, resulting in a sudden and strong emotional reaction that is often inappropriate to the nature of the threat. As a leader the art and practice of self-control is crucial, otherwise we may react in a manner that contributes uncivilly to the situation. An effective mechanism in the face of a perceived threatening situation, which can soothe our distressed feelings, is to mentally count to ten. When you feel your senses have been assaulted by inane acts or rude acts directed at you or others, count to ten. Mentally taking a deep breath and counting to ten recalibrates your response system and allows you halt the negative spiral that occurs when you lose control of your emotions, so that you can then reengage with a response to the discussion that's going on around you.

Key #14: Crush Chronic Offenders. The problem is that sometimes deviant workplace employees are so self-confident that they believe they are immune from the reach of the organization's justice system. To counteract this behavior you need to rush chronic offenders and hammer bad behaviors. Call the offenders on their behavior. Don't tolerate bad behavior. Why? Because behaviors you put up with are the ones you end up with.

Do you remember how J. K. Rowling's fabulous series of Harry Potter books introduced us to the Dementor? The Dementor is a creature whose presence is unconsciously felt more so than consciously identified. Likewise, aggressive and hostile employees are felt as much as they are seen or experienced. They can undermine safety and lower productivity because they cause their colleagues to become hyper vigilant in their presence, and respond to their presence by disengaging from the conversation and assuming the "flight or fight" mentality.

Experience has shown us that anxious employees are neither productive nor creative and their personal affect is limited. Bad behaviors perpetrated by your resident Dementor also interferes with the regular development of positive behaviors and a flexible culture. So what do you do? Crush bad behaviors! Crush the Dementor!

Quite simply bad behaviors ultimately destroy the life force of an organization and also sucks the soul out of the workforce. This is just the same way that humans react to Dementors in the Harry Potter books; where they forget any positive emotion or memory, and eventually fade away into a state of hopelessness, despair, and depression. In dealing with your resident Dementor be timely, and be consistent. To begin with you must never – under any circumstance – reward them for their bad behavior, as this will only serve to embolden them to continue on their soul destroying path. Supervise the Dementor more diligently so as to be able to pounce on deviant behavior as it occurs.

Confront bad behavior immediately and publicly as failure to do so can reinforce it, as both the perpetrator and other witnesses will note a lack of negative consequences for the behavior. Never assign a perpetrator as a mentor over another colleague, as they will simply groom another clone. They will feel more emboldened to continue their deviance when they have reinforcement and a follower. Exclude the Dementor from activities where creativity and innovation is required by assigning them to less visible aspects of the project, yet don't forget to reinforce the value of their lone efforts. Marginalize your Dementor from the core work yet keep them in sight of the goal post to both keep an eye on them, and leverage any residual utility they may have to contribute to the project. Consistently confront their cynicism and unhappiness and regularly inquire if they might be happier elsewhere. Encourage them to seek alternative employment in roles more suitable to their skills and abilities – or in the words of a Disney director, encourage them to recast themselves in a happier role elsewhere.

Key #15: Disagree Sans Being Disagreeable. The problem is that sometimes we contribute to or inflame an existing problem by how we respond. When there is a problem in the workplace, it can either be the result of an unresolved disagreement, or can present a situation that will eventually lead to disagreement. Seek first to understand. This is especially prudent advice for trained problem solvers, such as engineers and scientists, for whom it can be easy to jump to the conclusion that the situation was the result of a bad decision. Be certain why you disagree, and reflect upon whether the disagreement is based upon factual perspectives as opposed to personal disconnects.

Resist the rush to judgment and look for the common ground. Give others the benefit of the doubt. Inevitably when humans are involved in a disagreement there is more to the situation than first appears. Assume that there is some information that you are unaware of, so keep your mind open and look for clues. Once you have gained a firm degree of understanding of the situation you will also want to understand your contributing role in the disagreement. How have you directly or indirectly contributed to the disagreement? Do you even have a role in resolving the disagreement? Once you have established both your contributing role and your resolving role you can more effectively engage and positively influence the situation. Raise your concerns and insights to those who are authentically involved in the disagreement, making sure that your perspective has been heard and understood. In communicating your perspective you should void judgmental or inflammatory language and leave out the drama. If you are not the designated source for resolution, then leave the situation alone and move on. When those above you choose to act you can be assured that you have provided them the information that you have. You can disagree with the situation or the approach to resolution, without being disagreeable or uncivil. Unless life or limb or employee safety is at stake you do not have to go to war with the decision makers to enforce your perspective.

Key #16: Don't Be An Ass. The problem is that sometimes YOU are the problem. And perhaps you have also met that guy or gal in your professional life who fits the bill. We will refrain from any further pejorative language here as this book is about creating a civil workplace after all. But sometimes it's just you that is causing the problem. The significance of this strategy is that there is an opportunity for self-reflection, and specifically to call yourself out. The Don't Be an Ass strategy has two purposes;

- #1 To recognize that you don't have to be so quick to attribute pejorative titles and deviant behaviors to another, and

- #2 check your own self to see if you are more deserving of the title, than perhaps you give yourself credit for.

Key #17: Don't Excuse Powerful Offenders. The problem is that we often tolerate deviant behaviors in our star performers as we labor under the false belief that their contribution is more valuable to the organization than that of our other performers. This line of thinking however, represents a false economy. Because the spillover or toxic effect of one high performer affects the organizational and individual wellbeing beyond the immediate site of the behavior and contaminates of a huge array of other people, including employees, corporate stakeholders, and customers and consumers.

Behaviors that contribute to workplace incivility is not easily contained and knows no boundaries. It is not curtailed by some magical barrier just because it is perpetrated by the office rainmaker. Be consistent and apply the same standards of justice to every employee, especially the high performers, the mega producers, and the organizational wunderkinds. Perceived imbalance in the application of organizational justice will only serve to create additional incivility spiral, and will diminish employee affect, creativity, and innovation.

Key #18: Empathize Vs. Sympathize. The problem is that the target of incivility cannot rely on your support or intercession if you sympathize with their predicament, rather than empathize with it. Empathy can be explained as a person's ability to recognize and share the emotions of another person or group of people and involves understanding another's situation from their perspective, including understanding his emotions and his distress.

The terms empathy and sympathy are often used interchangeably but in error, although they are distinctly different. Sympathy is the reaction to the plight of others and reflects a feeling of care and concern for someone, accompanied by a desire for them to be better. However, sympathy, in contrast with empathy, does not involve a shared perspective or shared emotions. When a leader or a manager can empathize with the target of workplace incivility, and recognize and share understanding of the emotional harm caused to the employee everyone wins. They will be more motivated and influential in addressing the deviant organizational dynamic that has caused harm to the employee and the employee will feel that justice is possible.

Key #19: Employ Emotional Intelligence. Emotional intelligence is a characteristic within each of us that is sometimes elusive, yet its effect and affect is perceptible in the life we live. Emotional intelligence effects the quality of our worklife. It affects how we manage our behavior, negotiate for our needs, navigate social complexities, and manage interpersonal relationships that achieve or hinder positive outcomes. Emotional intelligence is derived from four core skills (self-awareness, self-management, social awareness, and social competence) within the two significant worklife competencies, namely personal competence and social competence. When you learn about EI and learn how to recognize and understand yours and others emotions, you can use the information to navigate the workplace and avoid, mitigate or manage incidents of workplace incivility. EI improves job performance and is found within the inventory of advanced leadership skills among known successful leaders. Personal competence includes self-awareness and self-management skills, which keep you aware of your emotions, and helps to manage your behaviors and positively direct your outcomes. Social awareness and relationship management skills enable you to be aware of other people's moods, behavior, and motives, and serve as the foundation for building and improving the quality of your relationships. Fear not, because IQ, unlike EQ which is innate, can be learned and developed over time.

Key #20: Examine Conflict. The problem is we are conditioned to respond to or deal with conflict as if the conflict itself was the problem, without understanding that conflict is merely a symptom of some other underlying disagreement.

The art of conflict management involves exploring and understanding what is behind the conflict. Typically there are one, two or even three reasons behind interpersonal conflict in the workplace, and each or all of these reasons can give rise to workplace incivility. The three primary reasons behind workplace conflict are a lack of clarity, a relationship issues, and/or resistance to direction or change. When you take the time to examine which of the three contributors are at play you can then begin to work towards resolving the conflict.

Key #21: Examine Influence. The problem is that most people have no idea how influence works, or why some people are more influential than others. Workplace incivility or civil behaviors can be spread through the influence of others. By understanding the art of influence you can learn to leverage its power to promote a positive culture. Positive influence can be used to mitigate and manage the impact of workplace deviance. Influence matters for effective leadership and influencing skills can be learned. And they are useful for leaders and managers who aspire to achieve greater influence within their work life and workplace. Influence can be used to overcome obstacles and build effective long-term relationships. Professional success also depends on your ability to effectively influence both your direct reports and the people over whom you have no direct authority, such as peers and external stakeholders.

The ability to influence is an essential skill of leadership, however, influence is more art than science, and it can be difficult to accomplish without some study, reflection, and practice. A crash course in influence begins with recognizing that there are five categories of influence. These categories include; #1. Asserting - that we insist that our ideas be heard over others and we challenge those others. #2. Bridging - that we connect with others, build relationships and coalitions through listening and understanding. #3.

Convincing - that we submit our ideas and our point of view along with logical reasons to convince others. #4. Inspiring - that we advocate and champion for our position and inspire others to accept a shared sense of purpose. #5. Negotiating - that we look for concessions and compromises to achieve outcomes that satisfy our greater interest.

Key #21. Understand Your Influencing Style. As with most things in our work life and with the workplace our journey into influence begins with self-awareness. What is your dominant type of influencing behavior? Do you exhibit a preference to assert, bridge, convince, inspire, or negotiate? Do you tend to apply the same approach to every domain, situation, or individual? Becoming aware of and understanding your natural influencing inclination is a good place to start.

If you're not sure, practice some self-reflection by catching yourself in the act of influencing and record both the context and the exhibited style. You may also find it useful to observe the same behaviors in others and reflect upon their preferred style and also how they employ influence.

Whether you are leading, following, and/or collaborating, chances are you need to influence others to be successful in your professional endeavors. The key is knowing which influencing approach to use in any given situation, all the while having the confidence in your technique as you execute your influencing strategy.

Key #22: Explain Yourself. The problem is you hire someone new to the team or workgroup, then you don't explain to them the cultural norms and behavior expectations as you assume that they will already know how to behave civilly in the workplace. Begin with the end in mind and how your business creates value and what the organizations' value proposition is. Then explain how their role creates value. After the employee understands the organization and their role, you must follow up with the specifics about the why of why you hired them. Employees are usually hired for one or two specific reasons, but oftentimes the reasons get lost in the hubris of the recruitment, interview, and onboarding process. Most importantly you should reinforce the connection between their skills, knowledge, ability, attitude, and their potential as an affect worker relative to the expected behaviors of the organization. When you explain yourself and the reasons behind why bring a new member onto your team you not only give them the performance expectation for the job but you also share with them your expected behaviors for the assignment.

Tell them what it was you saw in them that helped you make your hiring decision. Few statements are more motivating or can set the stage for achieving workplace civility better than, "I hired you because you exude positive leadership attributes... and we're all counting on you to positively affect the rise of civil behaviors among the rest of our team."

Key #23: Explore Cultures. The problem is that we don't always understand or appreciate cultural differences; which can create misunderstandings leading to acts of incivility. Intercultural communication challenges are present in our interdependent and global world, where advances in technology have reduced time and space, and we are now instantaneously connected to people from other countries. Cross-cultural communication skills are necessary to interact with international colleagues and customers. To be an effective communicator in an international business world, it is essential to understand the different cultural dynamics and behavior styles. The first challenge for individuals is to overcome ethnocentrism, which is the tendency to evaluate other cultures as inferior to our own. This skill can be learned through researching other cultures.

Key #24: Explore Unconscious Bias. The problem is that we all have biases that we are unaware of – yes, all of us, and our biases can influence worklife decisions and interpersonal interactions, leading to unintended uncivil behaviors towards others. As human beings we sometimes make choices that discriminate against one group in favor of another, without even realizing that we do it, even though we are absolutely convinced of our own fairness and that we are never biased in our decision-making.

Research has shown that every one of us is biased toward something, somebody, or some group - it's just the way we are wired. Each one of us has a group with whom we are aware that we feel uncomfortable, yet these conscious biases are minimal in comparison to the unconscious schemes that impact our thinking daily. Unconscious perceptions govern many of the most significant judgments we make, which impact the lives of many people in untold ways. By exploring the phenomenon of unconscious bias, we can learn to recognize that our thinking can be biased without us knowing it. One way to avoid contributing to workplace incivility is to establish a regular activity of 'checking our biases' and to practice reframing our workplace conversations to focus on fairness and respect and avoid harming others.

Key #25: Explore White Space. The problem is that within our workplace organizations we don't always understand the relationships between people and functions, or between the various boxes across the organizational chart. Without understanding the lay of the land we can misdiagnose organizational problems, which in turn can exacerbate systemic incivility issues and create havoc for our workgroup. Our eyes are accustomed to first looking for what we know and understand, without regard for the white space on the organization chart – which is empty after all, right?

The White Space of your organization chart can be more treacherous to the pursuit of a high-performance culture than any single malignant manager, underperforming department, or failing workgroup. Unregulated White Space can undermine your high-performance expectations towards creating superior business results. Confronting the myth that White Space on the organization chart is empty is your first step to leading and influencing beyond your functional domain. Executive presence begins with being 'present' outside of your own functional space and comfort zone. The crash course in exploring and managing white space includes;

Tip #1. Accept that understanding the unseen function of your organization's White Space is a critical aspect of your broader leadership purpose.

Tip # 2. Become familiar with the nature of actors engaged in your organizations' White Space, and understand the extent of their reach and influence.

Tip #3. Develop an understanding of the current process handoffs and multidirectional activity, and join with other leaders, managers, and influencers to build bridges through process improvements strategies, towards minimizing organizational disharmony within the White Space and in adjacent organizational boxes.

Tip # 4. Communicate and connect with the leaders, teams, and operational units across the White Space divide, towards expanding your area of influence.

Tip # 5. Stay alert to the health and wellbeing of the entire eco-system, even in the farthest reaches of the organizational White Space, and you will become adept at being responsive to emerging organizational threats and demands, towards creating a high-performance organization.

Key #26: Express Your Values. The problem is that most of us are confident in expressing performance expectations. However, we seldom express behavior expectations. Although we are fully aware of our personal and professional values, we seldom articulate them to our friends and colleagues. An unconventional workplace culture improvement strategy would be to openly share our values with our colleagues and our team, as a means to create behavior expectations and to raise the bar for positive workplace behaviors. Our personal values might include our attitude toward the environment, the disfranchised, our community, education, etc. Professional values reflect a balance between helping the organization achieve performance goals and our personal contribution to corporate social responsibility.

Many years ago I acquired a new leader who held a town hall for his entire workforce for the sole purpose of telling us who he was, what he stood for, and what his values were. In the three years I worked for him he never once deviated from the persona he presented to us on day one – and during his tenure we endured a very civil and successful working environment. The gist of his value-sharing presentation, titled "Murphy on Murphy" (names changed to protect the innocent) was simply a reflection of what he stood for. I adapted his approach over the years and have used the following value-sharing tips to make my case to my new team as follows:

Tip #1. Accountability and Responsibility - when you mess up, own it and report it. Bad news does not improve with age.

Tip #2. Loyalty Counts - be there for the people who are there to support the organization - even when they screw up. Honesty and honest feedback are critical to loyalty.

Tip #3. Integrity Matters - don't compromise it or play games with the truth, as there is no coming back from a lie.

Tip #4. Gossip is the purview of idle minds - don't do it. Teamwork and trust is essential to successful performance. When we gossip about others, people listening eventually figure out that you are sniveling about them too. Negative comments defy secrecy and inevitably find their way back to the victim of gossip, and ultimately your reputation is marginalized. Remember what Mom use to say – if you have nothing nice to say then say nothing.

Tip #5. Professionalism Matters - and understanding and conforming to workplace norms of respect, civility, inclusion and engagement is the mark of a professional.

Key #27: Express Gratitude. The problem is we don't express gratitude often enough. I am who I am today because of the kindness and wisdom shared by some spectacular fellow worklife travelers, managers, leaders and bosses. I am certain that I have missed many opportunities to express my gratitude to the many great and humble, and kind, and concerned colleagues I have encountered in the course of my career. Oftentimes my best learning has come from others who were courageous enough to voice a different truth about my approach, strategy, skill level, behavior or attitude. I'm grateful for the supportive way they have given me feedback –

although I may not have said so at the time. Learning to express gratitude and acknowledge the various perspectives offered by your colleagues invites more opportunity to become aware of your blind spots.

No one is asking you to subvert your leadership responsibility, however creating a culture of gratitude when you receive feedback demonstrates to others your willingness to entertain other perspectives. This is true whether it be about your behavior, performance or strategy. As leaders we are co-creators of the destiny of our organization, especially as we lead, manage and influence the new affect worker. No longer can we simply conduct or direct performance, rather we are creating the environment where the affect worker can become the best he can be. When others stop telling us that we are getting in the way of their greatness then we have lost the ability to influence outcomes. I am grateful for your feedback!

Key #28: Be A Horrible Boss. The problem is that although we know what a horrible boss looks like and behaves like, we seldom recognize that sometimes we are behaving like that horrible boss. Bad bosses are the main cause for the rise of workplace incivility. In order to be considered successful in our work lives we must endure the shackles of 'superior leadership performance' and 'positive workplace cultural norms.' The pressure to become the most beloved leader or the most brilliant boss is enormous. We see evidence and instruction daily in a barrage of media forums and how-to blogs (even here in this book) about the variety of steps necessary to achieve this state of organizational and leadership bliss. Instead of figuring out how to be a great boss why not treat yourself to an imaginary day of being a horrible boss, simply for the purpose of knowing which behaviors can make bosses bad!

The following offers a crash course for how to behave like a horrible boss - although you can create your own list. Imagine what your day would be like if you were;

Tip#1: Always Be the Smartest Guy (Or Gal) In the Room. Great leaders are self-aware. The humility exercised by great leaders allows them to sit comfortably in the knowledge that they possess huge gaps in their skillset, which in turn permits them to solicit and accept input, knowledge, and wisdom from others. To become the best at being the worst leader you must assume that you already know everything you need to know about everything worth knowing – you do not need to solicit input from others, either peers or subordinates. Why? Because you already know everything and have each situation fully covered. To reinforce this truth you must chide and denigrate those who are foolhardy enough to attempt to influence the discussion or add to your conversation. Remember that humility is for sissies. Never ask for input or admit that others might have some value to add to the discussion.

Tip #2: Never Ever Praise - But Criticize frequently and publically. Praise and recognition is an integral part of a fruitful worklife - especially in our formative years. When the boss acknowledges our contribution (or the contribution of our team) or praises our effort, we understand that our effort has been validated and typically we are motivated to do more and be more. Sometimes the boss is critical of our work or our level of effort – however, when he/she is quick to praise and slow to criticize we are more open to the constructive critique - especially if it is delivered privately and we don't lose face in front of our peers. But for you to excel as an uber-bad boss and worthless leader you must endeavor to never praise your subordinates and to frequently criticize them in a variety of public forums. To be a great bad-boss you must not fear an audience when you heap criticism on your subordinates, for they will remember the lesson more fondly against the backdrop of their peers and colleagues who are looking on during the public the berating.

Tip#3: Be A Divisive Leader. Great leadership is about getting along with others. And getting along with others is the essence of getting ahead, because leadership success is underscored by strong cooperation skills. Organizational cooperation is about working or acting together for a common purpose or benefit of the company. Oftentimes bad bosses will promote the interests of their own team or unit at the expense of the organization, and their divisive behavior negatively influences the attitudes and behaviors of their subordinates – to the point that the workgroup becomes recognized as a pariah team. This failure to cooperate for the greater good however, is an excellent means for you to project your utter failing as a leader and also demonstrate your crummy boss skills. Just imagine if you could (for one day) lead your team as if they were a tribe on the game show SURVIVOR - where the goal is to win the prize at the expense of all the other teams.

Obviously the above instruction is written tongue-in-cheek, however whether you are leading, following, and/or collaborating, chances are you have never contemplated the need to develop skills to increase awareness of what it takes to behave as a bad leader or horrible boss. How often have you sat around with colleagues and bemoaned a horrible boss, or an incompetent leader, or told some comedic tale of leadership malfeasance? When you learn how to identify negative behaviors within your own leadership style, or within your organization that decrease morale, decrease productivity, or sabotage business goals through disregard and disrespect of others, you have begun your own personal journey to becoming a great leader and a great boss. Safe travels!

Key #29: Hog The Blame. The problem is that what we were good at got us to where we are today – and often that involved hogging the glory of our success without sharing the praise with others who helped us to succeed. Conversely, we sometimes shared the blame when things went south in our early career, without taking full responsibility for our role in the failure. As a reminder however, the actions and behaviors that got us to this point in our career typically won't serve to move us forward to more senior or executive level positions. An unconventional career advancement and workplace culture improvement strategy would be to always "hog the blame and share the glory". I cannot claim this wisdom as my own, as it was a gift given to me by a great boss many years ago.

If something went bad in a team project wherein he was the leader, he would take full responsibility for the project's failure. Conversely, if things went well he would share the glory, the rewards, and the recognition with the entire team. We all loved this guy!!! We would have followed him anywhere and we always wanted to work on his projects. When a project goes bad or fails to deliver according to plan don't be tempted to identify the several "culprits" from within the team, rather be the leader and accept responsibility. Conversely, when a project goes well you must refrain from self-promotion and humble-bragging and allow your team to gain fame and recognition for the group effort. On a side note you will obviously gain greater long-term benefit by sharing the credit than by hogging it to yourself.

Key #30: Know Why You Work. The problem is most people don't know the "why" of why they work, and without clarity of purpose in their worklife they succumb to the distraction of daily nuisances; and oftentimes they find themselves contributing to poor workplace behaviors such as overt incivility, gossip, drama, conflict, and withholding their best effort. Understanding the "why" of why we work is both a leadership and an influencing trait, reflecting deep self-awareness, and a purposeful awareness of others. Also understanding the "why" of why your team member's work helps to improve team relationships. In following Maslow's hierarchy of needs we can understand that work provides for our basic physiological and safety needs, and also meets our interpersonal needs, which satisfies our feelings of belongingness. As human beings we also need to feel a sense of belonging and acceptance among our social groups and to feel respected and accepted and valued by others.

The true why of why we work is for reasons of self-actualization and to satisfy the fundamental belief that what we can be, we must become. This reason to work refers us each achieving our full potential and the realization of that potential. When we reflect upon our own reasons for working and seek to understand others' reasons for working we come to accept that each of us are at a different place in our worklife journey. Knowing where we are and accepting where others are in this human journey allows us to be kinder, more accepting, less judgmental and potentially more civil in our work lives and towards our fellow workers.

Key #31: Know Yourself. The problem is that we are oftentimes so busy that we don't take the time to 'know' ourselves. This lack of clarity can lead to worklife behaviors that are contrary to a civil workplace. Take time to reflect on who you are as a person, colleague, leader and manager. Learn to identify negative behaviors within your professional life, your leadership style, or your organizational persona that decrease morale, productivity, or sabotage your business goals through disregard and disrespect of others.

Knowing yourself becomes the first step towards making improvements in your relationship with others. Self-awareness can be achieved through self-reflection, feedback and coaching and each method offers very different value, depending upon where you are on your worklife journey.

Key #32: Pursue Leadership Preparedness. The problem is that as leaders we want to be better leaders so as to create better (and more civil) workplaces for our workgroup to excel; however we don't fully prepare for the task. As human beings we each aspire to become "better" and to achieve mastery, autonomy, and purpose in our worklife. Some of us make New Year's resolutions, while others just "hope" to be better bosses, employees, partners, spouses, or fellow travelers in this journey called life. Of the many parables we read about in our youth, *The Parable of the Sower,* provides us a strategy for becoming better leaders. The parable suggests that what matters most is not the seed or the idea that is planted, but the preparedness of the soil and the welcome it receives.

Typically, in olden days when the sower sowed his seed he would scatter it over a wide path by simply flinging handfuls of seed taken from his basket. He would then shallowly plough the soil to embed the seed. Contemporary farming allows for more precise planting, however the eventual fruitfulness of the seed still depends upon the nature and preparedness of the ground upon which it falls. As leaders we have a duty to both prepare ourselves, as well as to prepare those we are responsible to lead.

We gain authenticity in our leadership role when we have prepared for the task. As leaders we are bound to coach, teach, and mentor our work team, our volunteer organization and even our families. As we pursue a "better" version of ourselves we can help by taking some time to improve our focus and self-awareness. The triad of focus includes yourself, others, and the wider world. Over or under-focus on any one leg of the triad results in personal imbalance, limited ability to influence, and even professional failure. If you have limited self-focus or self-awareness you will have difficulty steering towards a desired goal.

If you have limited ability to focus on others, you will remain unconscious to the sinuous nature of relationships, and the interconnectivity of people and organizations. You will miss the destructive clues such as passive resistance, suspicion, distrust, or lack of engagement. If you have limited focus on the wider world, you will lack situational awareness and remain blind to external threats. You will be hit by global events long after your competitors have trimmed their sails. The key then is to accelerate your leadership capacity is by preparing your own self before you hope to effectively coach, teach and mentor others.

Key #33: Listen Hard. The problem is that oftentimes we don't listen to understand, rather we listen to make our next statement. When we listen harder we are less likely to act with incivility. Not listening is disrespectful and gives rise to feelings of personal disregard and professional minimization. Organizational relationships are complicated because we are all human beings - coming from many different cultural and individual backgrounds. Disagreements and conflict are bound to occur among staff members, between staff and management, and between partner organizations or customers. Bad feelings, relationship problems, destructive conflict, and inefficiencies result from the WAY that people listen to each other.

Listening skills are often lacking in leaders because they are not learned, resulting in unnecessary conflict and friction. Ironically, the word listen contains the same letters as the word silent. Active listening is an acquired skill and involves a conscious effort to listen not only the words that another person is saying but to understand the message intended in those words. Active listening is exhausting – simply because you must focus on the whole person and not allow yourself to be distracted by extraneous sounds or activities, or mentally developing alternative arguments, which you want to present as soon as the other person pauses to take a breath. Listen hard and listen close by listening silently – with an open mind and a closed mouth.

To become a better listener there are several techniques you can practice without being detected. To begin with you can employ minimal encouragers, which are the sounds you make to affirm that you are indeed listening – you already have this skill, especially when you are on the telephone! Just bring it forward into everyday conversation and reflect on the difference in the quality of conversation you have with other people. The encouraging sounds and words such as "uh Hum" or "Oh?" or "When?" allows others to know you are listening and quickly builds rapport and encourages the other person to provide even more information. Asking open-ended questions encourages the other person to say more; specifically asking questions that cannot be answered with a yes or no answer. Encouraging the other person by using the expression of *"Say more?"* is extremely powerful in eliciting more information while engaging your active listening skills. Paraphrasing also demonstrates active listening and it creates empathy and establishes rapport as it becomes more evident to the speaker that you are indeed listening and that you have heard and understood them.

Strategic pauses and silence are also effective listening techniques as most people are not comfortable with silence and as a student of effective listening you will find that it is to your advantage to keep the other person talking. You will learn more by being silent. As a final thought here is a wonderful quote on the power of listening by Stephen Covey, *"When you really listen to another person from their point of view, and reflect back to them that understanding, it's like giving them emotional oxygen."* So, listen hard!

Key #34: Rebuke Uncivil Behavior – Civilly. The problem is we often call the uncivil offender on their bad behavior in an uncivil manner, which belies our attempt to correct the bad behavior. Such a poor response gives rise to further unintended incivility spirals. For example calling the office 'dirtbag' a dirtbag, when we are addressing his behavior, does not lead to a positive outcome.

Key #35: Recognize Your Saboteur. The problem is that we don't always recognize the telltale signs of workplace sabotage, which can be significant as employees purposely extract revenge against the organization for perceived injustice associated with incidents of workplace incivility.

Employees engage in organizational "resistance" or sabotage for a variety of reasons, ranging from lack of understanding, through intellectual disagreement, to unconscious bias towards others ideas, or in response to prejudices. Several of the reasons may be motivated by several interrelated actions such as; (1) concern about impending change initiatives, (2) that leaders or managers are incompetent, or disliked, or untrustworthy, (3) the organization is not worthy of deeper engagement or contribution, (4) that the employee fears loss of face, standing, authority, control or influence, (5) that the employee is afraid of being found incompetent in the face of changes and now fears for their job security. Whatever the reasons underlying organizational resistance and sabotage, this aspect of workplace conflict can give rise to multiple incivility spirals if left unattended.

Key #36: Deal With Debbi Downer. The problem is that Debbie or Dave Downer is toxic to our worklife, and creates an endless number of incivility spirals which can suck the joy out of our day. You know that 'special' person who can only be happy when their unhappiness taints and torments everyone else around them. You have to deal with the toxic situation, so the first thing you need to do is keep your defenses up and don't let her drag you down into her misery cave.

Offer her the same listening etiquette as you would any other colleague, without succumbing to her misery, and you just may help her out of her misery. Use the listening techniques outlined above, however limit the time exposure for your own sake to a very short chat. And whatever you do don't be tempted to agree just to shut her up or to end the conversation quickly. Otherwise, you will get pulled into a negative vortex from which it will be very difficult to extract yourself. However, neither do you want to stay silent as this will infer agreement to Debbie or Dave and any other listeners.....so tactfully restore untruths and extremes to factual perspectives! And did I mention to keep your defenses up and not let her under your skin or in your head?

Key #37: Share Your Vision (Of Future Possibilities). The problem is that as leaders most of us never share our vision of future possibilities with others. However, we often attempt to share our own personal vision of the future without regard for co-creation or joint ownership of this future vision by our teams. By sharing our vision of future possibilities as opposed to presenting a future end-state as a fait-accompli, we are inviting others into the process of co-creating our mutual future state. Followers are hungry for leaders who can envision and articulate forward-looking possibilities, which then draws them into the exercise of co-creating the shared vision.

The ability to share your vision of future possibilities is the hallmark that distinguishes great leaders from others. The best way to lead your team into the uncertain, complex, and ambiguous future is to co-create a shared vision of what your joint future can be. Begin the co-creation process by connecting with each of your team on a personal level, and then work to be in the present moment with them to listen deeply and closely to their aspirations, hopes, wants, needs, and desires. The best leaders are then able to bring their team forward into the arena of future possibilities and co-create a shared vision towards which they can then plan and execute a strategy, goals and objectives, which they will accomplish together.

Key #38: Own Your Mistakes. The problem is that while we all make mistakes we don't always admit to them – even to ourselves. This life of ours is a journey, and in the workplace we are traveling in very close proximity with many other souls on their own worklife journey. Sometimes we don't show up as the best version of ourselves in the workplace, and this lesser version of us contributes to the negativity and incivility that makes the journey for ourselves and other travelers unpleasant. When you reflect on your behavior and realize that you have had a bad day where the lesser version of you shows up then own it! "A life spent making mistakes is not only more honorable, but more useful than a life spent doing nothing". - George Bernard Shaw (1856-1950).

Mentally own it by being aware of how you showed up, without rationalizing the why of your behavior. As a leader you can serve as a greater influence to your followers if you also own up about your bad behavior. Be specific when you own up and be apologetic. *"Jack – yesterday I behave badly and unprofessionally when I raised my voice and spoke to you in a discouraging manner. I was wrong and I apologize."* Remember, you only really 'own it' if you do something about it.

Key #39: Respect Personal Space. The problem is that each one of us has a different bubble or zone of personal space, so that we are not always aware of the discomfort we cause when we encroach upon another's personal space. Proxemics, or the study of the spatial requirements of humans, is different for each individual, yet there are general similarities among major cultural groups. The way we are accustomed to operating within our own personal space may be acceptable within our culture, yet considered either invasive or unfriendly within other cultures, as different cultures maintain different standards of personal space. Appreciating and recognizing these differences even within our own culture or workgroup can eliminate discomfort that our colleagues may feel if the interpersonal distance is either too large, or too small. We can see how personal space is also affected by a person's position in society or within our organization, with more affluent or highly placed individuals enjoying or securing a larger personal space.

The contemporary workspace has created a degree of difficulty with regards our desire for personal space. Specifically, if we work in a dense office of cubicles and open benching we find that we are more likely to invade each other's personal space. Even among the different generations at work we can observe different degrees of proximity between and among the different age groups. The point here is that all individuals have a personal space preference, which they may or may not be consciously aware of. However, when it is invaded they will display either consciously or unconsciously their discomfort. As leaders and managers we have to be hypervigilant about invading our subordinates' personal space as this one activity can contribute significantly to organizational unease and the rise of uncivil behavior.

Key #40: Say Thanks. The problem is that we are all so busy all the time that we very seldom remember to say "thank you." Yet these two simple words are probably the most powerful words in any employee's repertoire of skills that he can deploy to prevent, mitigate or manage the occurrence of incivility in his workplace. Saying "thank you" to our employees, colleagues, managers and leaders is not just polite, it is critical for the health and wellbeing of our workplace and our organization. A culture of respect and appreciation is the lubricant that keeps an organization running smoothly, especially during tumultuous periods.

The art of appreciation and the words "thank you" are the equivalent of adding WD40 lubricant to a complex machine with numerous moving parts. Saying "thank you" keeps the affect worker engaged and positively affecting the wellbeing and creativity of fellow workplace warriors. The simple "thank you" is not just for the front-line troops. As an executive leadership coach I have encountered many employees from various levels within their organization that desire to be acknowledged for their efforts. After all, the contemporary affect worker delivers his work effort within a 24/7 culture, or over longer work hours and weekends, which causes their lives to fall out of balance. Thanking them is the least we can do and personal appreciation goes a long way to stem otherwise deviant behavior among a team or workplace that is feeling underappreciated or exhausted.

When saying "thank you" be specific. For example: *"I appreciate how you handled that difficult customer in such a diplomatic way when you engaged with him and spent 10 minutes listening to his complaint. You could have ignored his ranting until he ran out of steam."* Thank people publically or send an e-mail to their boss about what they did that you valued. A "thank you" can also be used with clients, customers, and leaders above you. Even the Big Guy Boss appreciates a heartfelt "thank you" from his team – as many days he goes to bat for you guys and you won't ever know that he did it. Saying "thank you" builds trust and offsets the conditions that can lead to the rise of workplace incivility, so it is an incredible tool in everyone's hand.

Part Three: A Corporate Strategy For Civility

15. The Workplace Civility Matters© Program

The Purpose Of The Program

The goal in writing ***Let's Get Civil In The Workplace*** was two-fold; (1) to present and promote the concept that workplace civility is a pillar of effective organizational behavior, and (2) to present and promote the idea that workplace civility is a required leadership competency. The impetuous in writing ***Let's Get Civil In The Workplace*** resulted in part because of the insights that the

MCG Consulting Group has garnered through the series of workshops presented under the banner of the WORKPLACE CIVILITY MATTERS © program (www.WorkplaceCivilityMatters.com). The program is designed to help organizations deal with workplace incivility, build and sustain a healthy culture and establish positive cultures towards achieving a high performing organization.

Part 1 and Part 2 of the this book offers respectively a current view of the phenomenon of workplace incivility, and a menu of forty tips that leaders of organizations, H.R. managers, influencers, and individual workers can employ towards combating workplace incivility and creating and sustaining a civil workplace.

Six (6) Corporate Strategies Towards Building A Civil Workplace

1. Conduct a Workplace Civility Assessment Survey©
2. Developing or updating your organizational or corporate strategy
3. Develop a civility keynote speaker's program
4. Develop and present experiential workshops for teams of leaders and influencers,
5. Train and develop internal trainers and civility ambassadors
6. Develop individual and group executive coaching

Six Strategies Towards Building A Civil Workplace

Strategy #1: Conducting an organizational wide workplace civility assessment survey to understand the prevalence and impact of workplace incivility and assess employee propensity towards embracing new behaviors towards creating a more civil workplace.

Strategy # 2: Developing or updating your organizational or corporate strategy and publishing your strategic planning outcomes to include a public value statement on workplace civility. Also publish a leadership development strategy that includes the concept that workplace civility is both a pillar of effective organizational behavior, and a required leadership competency.

Strategy #3: Develop a civility keynote speaker's program and invite into your organization speakers to present to individual workgroups and at organization-wide events. Civility speakers should address presentations on the negative impact of workplace incivility and the positive impact of the pursuit of a civil workplace. By creating awareness among the members of your workforce you will begin to plant the seed of a more positive culture and a more civil workforce leading to improved organizational outcomes.

Strategy #4: Develop and present experiential workshops for teams of leaders and influencers, and specific work units to explore, address and resolve group issues around workplace incivility and negative culture.

Strategy #5: Train and develop internal trainers and civility ambassadors (practitioners) to help organizations and work groups build positive cultures, and provide tools and information for individuals who can benefit from enhanced self-awareness and awareness of others, so as to develop their own ability to behave with civility.

Strategy #6: Developing individual and group executive coaching programs to address specific issues around deviant workplace behaviors and to create an awareness of civility as a leadership competency towards improving leadership capacity and executive presence.

16. Incivility Impacts Performance Outcomes.

The behaviors that contribute to workplace incivility represent a distinct point along the continuum of deviant workplace behavior and generally incorporates the element of interpersonal focus between one individual and another or a group of others. However, the target of incivility typically responds to the assault by seeking retribution against the organization. Logically then the organization wants to manage the situation to mitigate or eliminate acts of incivility so as to achieve desired performance outcomes and protect the bottom-line.

Research reflects that 96 to 99 percent of all employees, including our colleagues and ourselves, have experienced incivility firsthand. Some incivility instigators are genuinely unaware that they have behaved uncivilly, while others are known for their recurring acts of incivility; where they either act with reckless disregard or with malicious intent to cause offense to others in the workplace. However, if you know the right tactics and strategy, you can deflect, mitigate, and eliminate workplace incivility effectively (and perhaps lead and manage better organizations while you are at it).

What is the Payoff?

The payoff or return on investment for increased awareness of the phenomenon of workplace incivility, and acquiring knowledge of how to create a positive culture imbued with workplace civility is high for both organizations and individuals.

Organizations benefit from being able to count on a strong and positive culture with tools to manage conflict, communicate effectively, motivate team members, and sustain high-performance during periods of growth and change; which in turn gives them a competitive advantage when compared to organizations with little or no understanding about how to create or sustain a civil workplace. Civil organizations also gain from lower levels of counterproductive behavior during periods of ambiguity and uncertainty, and can expect a marked increase in organizational and corporate reputation as observed by external stakeholders.

Individuals benefit from being able to achieve their own worklife goals of autonomy, mastery and purpose in the midst of uncertainty with less conflict or impact from incivility, leading to greater personal autonomy and professional satisfaction.

What Can We Do?

Through employee surveys and organizational assessment, training and increased awareness of self and others, individuals and organizations can learn to understand, manage, and strengthen their own responses to workplace incivility. In turn, this increased awareness helps organizations and individuals build a stronger and more civil culture and more effective teams, which are crucial to building high performing organizations and achieving a competitive advantage.

17. Details Of The Six Strategies

The following chapter offers a more extensive explanation of the six corporate strategies that an organization can employ towards developing and executing a cultural improvement strategy leading to a more civil workplace.

Corporate Strategy #1:

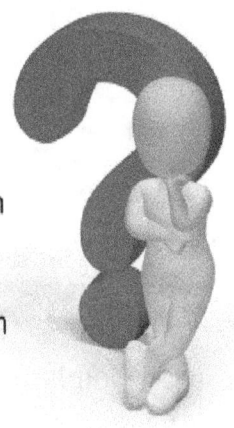

What Is The State Of Your Organization?

• Workplace incivility contributes to diminished organizational commitment and performance outcomes.

• Workplace incivility does not happen in a vacuum, as it appears to be a consequence of the deterioration of civility and the decline of trust within society in general.

www.WorkplaceCivilityMatters.com 2016   6

What Is The State Of Your Organization?

Strategy #1 includes conducting an organizational wide workplace civility assessment survey to explore and understand the prevalence and impact of workplace incivility and assess employee propensity towards embracing new behaviors leading to creating a more civil workplace.

What Is The Workplace Civility Assessment Survey©?

- The **WCAS©** instrument serves two purposes;
  - 1st - to create an immediate awareness of and name otherwise ambiguous deviant workplace behaviors.
    - .... the participants became aware of the phenomenon workplace incivility during the moments of inquiry
    - and are thus presented with new knowledge upon which to reflect and act towards creating a more civil workplace
  - 2nd - to identify the several root causes of workplace incivility

www.WorkplaceCivilityMatters.com 2016

What Is The Workplace Civility Assessment Survey©

The Workplace Civility Matters© program includes a comprehensive workplace and work group qualitative assessment and surveys to determine the baseline awareness of, existence of, and understanding of the impact of uncivil behaviors upon your organization.

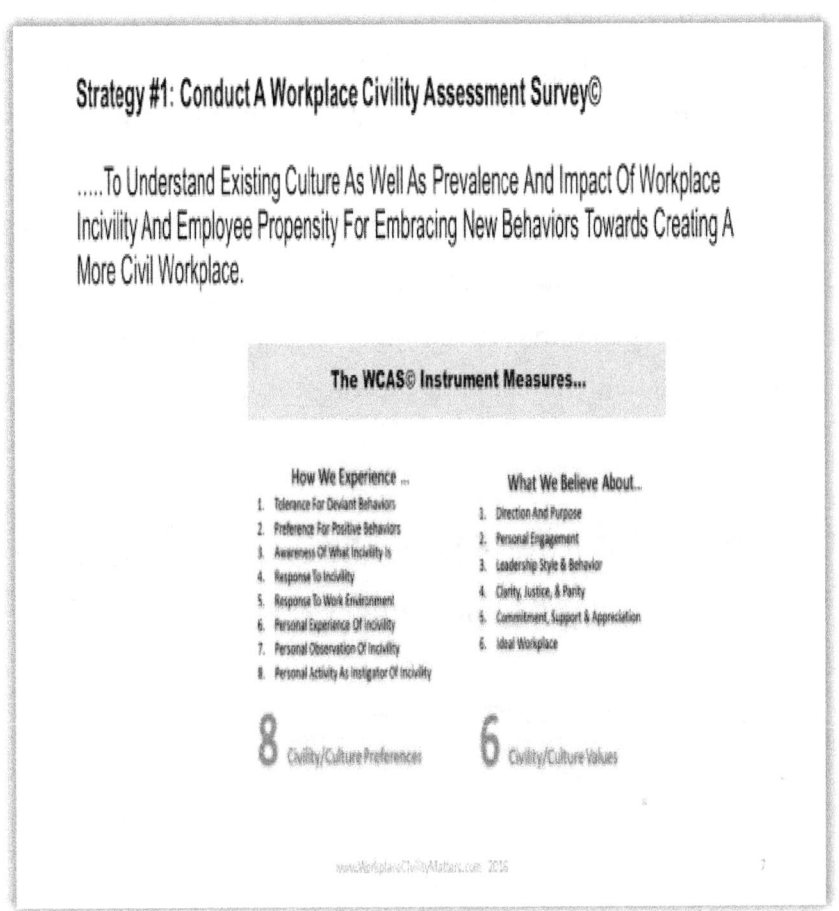

Explaining The WCAS©

The Workplace Civility Matters© program includes the Workplace Civility Assessment Survey© (WCAS©), which is designed to measure the extent to which incivility appears to be a problem in workplace settings (small groups, large teams, functional areas, cross large organizations), and to assess your employees' propensity for developing and sustaining workplace civility as a cultural norm. The survey instrument itself serves two purposes;

The first purpose serves to create an immediate awareness of and to name the otherwise unnamed or ambiguous deviant workplace behaviors. Otherwise stated, through the survey process the participants became aware of the phenomenon workplace incivility during the moments of inquiry, and are thus presented with new insight upon which to act towards creating a civil workplace.

WCAS© Is A Workplace And Worklife Culture And Civility Assessment

- Baseline awareness of, existence of, and understanding of, the impact of uncivil behaviors upon your organization.

- The outcome of the survey leads to identifying appropriate strategies, which help individuals and organizations effectively manage and alter the workplace environment and work-life towards a happier, healthier, and more effective culture.

- Examines 8 Preferences and 6 Values

More About The WCAS©

The second purpose of the workplace civility assessment survey is more concrete. Through extensive research, study, and practitioner experience, we have identified the several root causes of workplace incivility and the results of the survey will illuminate the presence of these specific areas of concern. This insight will provide a framework upon which to developed appropriate strategies to effectively manage and alter the workplace environment and work-life towards a happier, healthier and more effective culture.

Through Assessment Of Culture You Can Also Begin To Lay The Foundation To Generate Solutions...

✓ Create Awareness

✓ Demonstrate Commitment

✓ Achieving Buy-in

✓ Manage Incivility

✓ Deter Gateway Behaviors

✓ Begin To Establish A Positive Culture

✓ Positively Impact Your Organization

www.WorkplaceCivilityMatters.com 2016

WCAS© Outcomes

The results of the comprehensive survey can be employed to develop an organizational-wide civility response mechanism, towards establishing civility as a cultural norm while positively impacting organizational performance and business outcomes.

The WCAS survey consists of approx. 130 questions and is made available electronically to your employees and their input is anonymous.

The WCAS© Instrument Measures...

How We Experience ...

1. Tolerance For Deviant Behaviors
2. Preference For Positive Behaviors
3. Awareness Of What Incivility Is
4. Response To Incivility
5. Response To Work Environment
6. Personal Experience Of Incivility
7. Personal Observation Of Incivility
8. Personal Activity As Instigator Of Incivility

8 Civility/Culture Preferences

What We Believe About...

1. Direction And Purpose
2. Personal Engagement
3. Leadership Style & Behavior
4. Clarity, Justice, & Parity
5. Commitment, Support & Appreciation
6. Ideal Workplace

6 Civility/Culture Values

www.WorkplaceCivilityMatters.com 2016

What The WCAS© Measures

The survey remains open and available for a designated period of time and the results and can be consolidated and returned to you rapidly. The survey sections addressing a variety of culture and engagement topics, including employee sensitivity to deviant behaviors, employee response to workplace incivility, organizational impact of current bad behaviors, uncovering source and root cause of incivility, and identifying employee propensity for change and embracing civility as a cultural norm.

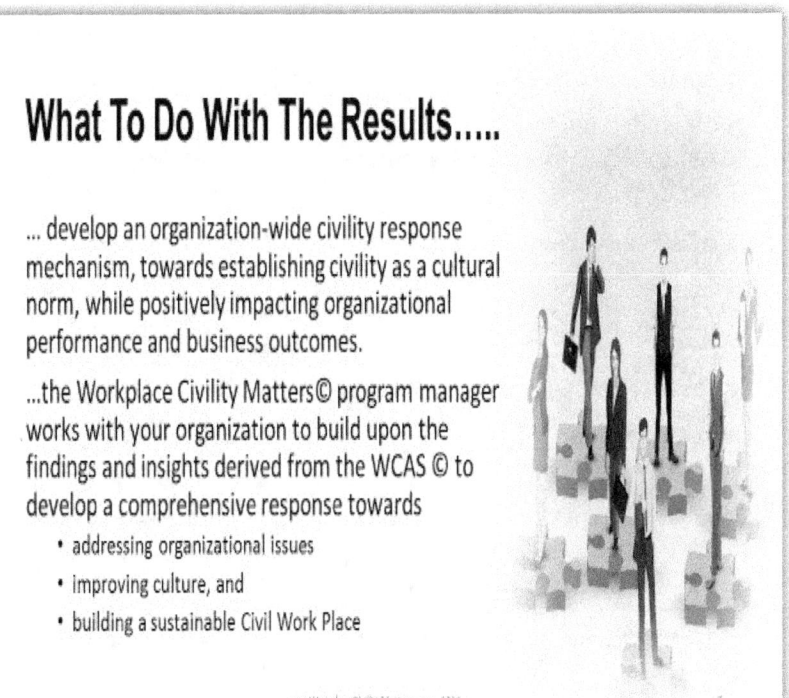

What To Do With The Results

The results of the survey can serve to highlight specific problem areas within your organization and serve as a guide for future training, development, speaking and seminar or webinar engagements, leadership development and executive coaching programs.

Different Ways The WCAS© Can Be Used?

Training and Development - Understand your culture/civility needs and challenges before you prioritize scarce T&D dollars.

Baselining - Develop a comprehensive baseline by department or group of current cultural/civility health.

Culture Change - Develop a common operating perspective before executing a civility/cultural improvement strategy.

Restructuring - Conduct SWOT analysis of culture and deviant behavior, and establish employee trust in leadership and propensity for change.

Organizational Transitions - Target and prioritize culture/civility challenges during transition

Leadership Changes - Gain an accurate and real-time assessment of the health and wellbeing of your new assignment/organization/workgroup.

Explore/Understand - When you suddenly have a spate of complaints, "accidents", absenteeism, or attrition – use the survey to look behind the mirror and check out what's going on.

Team Building/Group Coaching – Of all the ways to employ the WCAS® using it in conjunction with a team building or group coaching session delivers phenomenal results as the combination address team dynamics, interpersonal issues, communication challenges, leadership capacity and executive presence.

Different Ways The WCAS© Can Be Used

18. Corporate Strategy # 2:

Strategy # 2: Develop Or Update Your Organizational Or Corporate Strategy

- Develop or update your organizational or corporate strategy (mission, vision, goals, objectives) and publish your strategic outcomes
  - to include a value statement on workplace civility
  - and a leadership development strategy that includes the concept that workplace civility
  - is a pillar of effective organizational behavior, and a required leadership competency
- WCM© can facilitate!

www.WorkplaceCIVILityMatters.com 2016

Strategy #2

Developing or updating your organizational or corporate strategy and publishing your strategic planning outcomes to include a public value statement on workplace civility, and a leadership development strategy that includes the concept that workplace civility is a pillar of effective organizational behavior, and is a required leadership competency. Many strategic planning efforts run aground because of the failure to correctly plan and implement. Why does this happen?

Having facilitated many strategic planning off-sites over the years, we've identified five steps to help successfully plan, design, execute and follow-up on your strategic planning workshop.

Tip #1. Establish and Clarify Purpose. Just as in the art of strategic planning itself the execution of the strategic planning offsite falls under the same axiom – which is that when we fail to plan, we also plan to fail! Of course, most effective organizations spend time and energy creating plans for the near and long term. Through the MCG Consulting Group list of offerings we help to not to only establish a clear sense of direction and purpose towards identifying and achieving preferred performance outcomes, we also help to establish the strategic planning workshop charter which identifies workplace civility as a core organizational value, and establish it as a cornerstone of the strategic planning process. This charter will help your organization pull together and create the commitment and consensus necessary to execute your preferred business strategy with civility as a core value. Having a clear mission, vision, goals, objectives, cultural norms, and operating plan built around the values of civility permits the whole organization to understand where you're headed and how civility as a cultural norm aligns with the bottom-line and preferred business outcomes.

Tip #2. Purposeful Preplanning. Generally a recurring strategic planning offsite begins many weeks ahead with a series of activities that include:

•Development of a planning framework with phases and stages of events along the process.

•Identification and invitation of the participants, including (1) employees, subject matter experts, and management executives to work through development of the various strategies, followed by the (2) executive committee to review and approve the final strategy.

•Preliminary groundwork to call for, gather, and assess data on the current status of the organization, and anticipated goals and strategies towards future business outcomes.

•Establishment of framework for chartering the various follow-up activities that will your convert concepts into action plans.

•Decision to source and hire an external meeting facilitator to help achieve strategic planning offsite outcomes.

Tip #3: Skilled Facilitation. To avoid any undue influence or conflict of interest we recommend sourcing an independent external facilitator. This is the time when you need someone outside of the organization to help frame the discussion around civility as a pillar of the organizations' strategy and to help create a cohesive process, guiding participants through challenging conversations and decisions, without losing focus on the value of civility. When selecting a strategic planning facilitator, choose someone with skills in guiding group interaction and invoking positive behaviors as a core value.

19. Corporate Strategy #3

Strategy #3

Developing a civility keynote speaker's program to bring into your organization speakers who will present (either by seminar or webinar) to individual workgroups and at organization-wide events.

Civility speakers should address presentations on the negative impact of workplace incivility and the positive impact of the pursuit of a civil workplace. By creating awareness among the members of the workforce you will begin to plant the seed of a more positive culture leading to improved organizational outcomes.

The MCG Consulting Group offers a wide array keynote topics http://www.mcgconsultinggroup.com/training/ to enhance employee worklife and workplace optimization through the lens of a civil workplace. An onsite seminar offers a structure that is similar to a lecture or classroom style of learning. In this respect, the speaker or instructor shares information with the attendees, similar to how a teacher lectures a classroom full of students. As a participant you listen and learn from our experienced speakers. A short period for questions and answers is included at the conclusion of the presentation. A virtual webinar is similar to an onsite seminar, as the name webinar is derived from the expression Web-based seminar. The instruction is transmitted over the WEB using Video Conferencing Software. As a participant you listen and learn from our experienced speakers. A short period for questions and answers is included at the conclusion of the presentation.

20. Corporate Strategy #4:

Strategy # 4: Develop And Present Experiential Workshops For Teams Of Leaders And Influencers

- Develop and present experiential workshops
  - for teams of leaders and influencers
  - specific work units
- To explore, address, and resolve group issues around workplace incivility and creative a positive cultural intentions
- WCM© can develop/present bespoke or on-the-shelf workshops!

www.WorkplaceCivilityMatters.com 2016

7

Strategy #4

Developing and present experiential workshops for teams of leaders and influencers, or to specific work units to explore and conduct root cause analysis, or resolve group issues. Specific workgroup issues include workplace incivility, leadership capacity, trust building, organizational dynamics, reputation management, and employee support for corporate social responsibility initiatives.

An onsite workshop includes elements of a seminar, however more significantly the format also includes customized hands-on activities designed to accelerate individual and group learning. The interactive and customized format also serves to (1) more deeply engage each participant, (2) leverage adult learning preferences, (3) create group awareness, (4) build organizational bridges, and (5) strengthen the team dynamic. As a participant you and a specific number of attendees interact with our experienced facilitator in a workshop customized to your organization and group needs.

The MCG Consulting Group offers over 130 training workshops (http://www.mcgconsultinggroup.com/training) under six general headings towards building a civil workplace, and developing competent and confident leaders with strong leadership skills and executive presence.

- Soft skills: Behavior, EQ, Bias, Influence Training workshops
- Behavior and Response: Conflict, Stress, Communication, Listening, Bully, Civility, Chaos Training workshops.
- Ethics: Compliance and Ethics, Culture, Behavior Training workshops
- Leadership Training workshops
- Management Training workshops
- Business: Strategy, Mission, Process, Planning Training workshops

Chapter 21

21. Corporate Strategy #5

Strategy # 5: Train And Develop Internal Trainers And Civility Ambassadors

• Train and develop internal trainers and civility ambassadors (practitioners)

  • to help organizations and work groups build positive cultures, and

  • provide tools and information for individuals who can benefit from enhanced self-awareness and awareness of others so as

  • to develop their own ability to behave with civility.

• WCM© can provide training and program support with *the It Matters What Leaders Do series*

Strategy #5

Train and develop internal trainers and civility ambassadors (practitioners) to help organizations and work groups build positive cultures, and provide tools and information for individuals who can benefit from enhanced self-awareness and awareness of others to develop their own ability to behave with civility. The MCG

Consulting Group also offers a train-the-trainer program in all aspects of the Workplace Civility Matters© program.

Civility Ambassadors Is A Self-Directed Agency Program

What It Does

1. Creates awareness
2. Stimulates conversation
3. Directed reading
4. Invokes civil behavior
5. Leadership platform
6. Values platform

How It Works

1. Launch by Leader, who presents tailored WCM© brief
2. Ambassador distributes weekly
   1. What Leaders Do post...
   2. Civility/Culture article...
3. Managers/Supervisors build upon
4. Employees engage in discussion...

www.WorkplaceCivilityMatters.com 2016   7

The Civility Ambassadors Program

Training internal trainers and civility ambassadors (practitioners) helps organizations and work groups build positive cultures using internal resources, and provides tools and information for individuals who can benefit from enhanced self-awareness and awareness of others to develop their own ability to behave with civility.

It Matters What Leaders Do

Our highly trained and experienced civility coaching team is continually researching and learning, updating our materials, and sharing new information with our civility ambassadors and practitioners. Our small and flexible operation allows us to be extremely responsive to both partner and client needs.

22. Corporate Strategy #6

Strategy # 6: Deliver Individual And Group Executive Coaching

- Developing individual and group executive coaching programs
  - to address specific issues around deviant workplace behaviors and
  - to create an awareness of civility as a leadership competency towards
  - improving leadership capacity and executive presence.
- WCM© can provide individual and group executive coaching

www.WorkplaceCivilityMatters.com 2016

Individual And Group Executive Coaching

Source and develop individual and group executive coaching programs to address specific issues around deviant workplace behaviors and to create an awareness of civility as a leadership competency towards improving leadership capacity and executive presence. Leaders, managers, influencers and H.R. Directors hire an

Executive Leadership Coach for themselves and members of their organization when there is a need for development in one of several areas:

- ✓ Gifted leaders who want to sustain and enhance their leadership and commutation skills.
- ✓ Aspiring leaders who want to grow their leadership capacity and become great leaders.
- ✓ Strategic thinkers who want to navigate uncertainty and take advantage of yet-to-be explored opportunities.
- ✓ Seasoned leaders seeking work/life balance or preparing for life transitions.
- ✓ Emerging executives seeking enhanced executive presence in their newly assigned leadership roles.
- ✓ Technical experts seeking to influence broader conversations within their organization or worklife.
- ✓ Confident Leaders who want to grow and develop competent and confident future leaders.

23. Final Thoughts

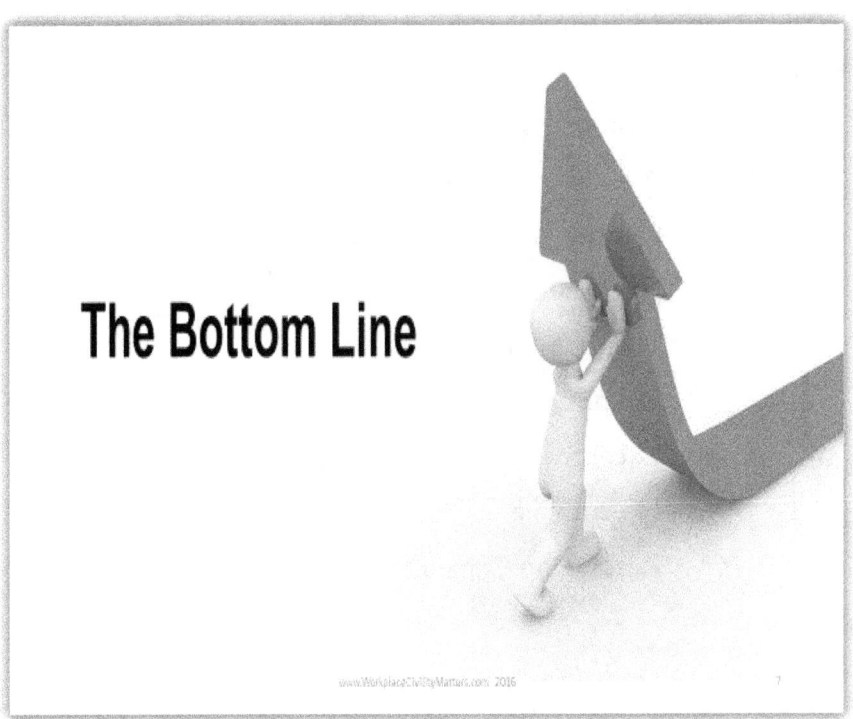

The Bottom Line

Dr Martina Carroll-Garrison, as a Professionally Certified Coach offers coaching support to individuals and teams or groups who are wrestling with behaviors that hold them back or interfere with desired performance outcomes.

As an executive leadership coach I recognize that certain behaviors that have helped you to become successful today may be standing in the way of tomorrow's professional advancement. I can coach you to identify and laser-in on specific aspects of your story, which may be holding you back - so that you can move forward. The focus can be on:

- ✓ Awareness of self
- ✓ Awareness of others
- ✓ Civility as a cultural norm
- ✓ Goal setting
- ✓ Team building
- ✓ Simplify the complex
- ✓ Executive decision-making
- ✓ Executive presence
- ✓ Leadership Capacity

Epilogue…

Workplace Civility Matters © helps to...

✓ … enhance employee wellbeing and engagement
✓ … manage workplace incivility
✓ … deter gateway behaviors that lead to workplace violence
✓ … establish and sustain a positive culture
✓ … create a civil work environment
✓ … enable desired performance outcome
✓ … positively impact the bottom-line of organization

The Program Helps To....

Workplace Civility Matters! Workplace Incivility Sucks! You have the power to do something about it! Recall if you will that we began this book by presenting the idea that work has independent value for you and your colleagues as workers, beyond the basics of shelter, subsistence, and survival. We declared that each worker aspires to perform his work in harmony with his surroundings and with his fellow workers. We have now documented and recognized that regardless of the trade or the profession, it is not a common truth that today's workplace offers such harmony to each worker.

Uncivil behaviors found within the greater society have taken hold within the contemporary workplace. *Let's Get Civil In The Workplace* examined the impact that uncivil behaviors have on our workplaces and within our work lives. We have come to understand the emotional, professional, social, and spiritual toll that workplace incivility has on each of us at a very personal level, as well as on our work family and our friends. For each of us who have witnessed or endured a worklife disrupted by uncivil behavior this book is our declaration of war. We are no longer willing to accept workplace incivility in our businesses and organizations!

Let's Get Civil In The Workplace explored three aspects of the worklife; Firstly we reviewed the rise of deviant behaviors as a consequence of social changes, decline in trust as a universal value, changes in the workplace as a result of global changes and finally changes in demands and expectations place upon the contemporary worker. Secondly we reviewed the antithesis of workplace incivility, which included the parameters of workplace civility, as preferred organizational behavior, and we then examined forty strategies that each employee can use towards creating a more civil workplace. Thirdly we examined six overarching strategies that an organization can employ from a corporate perspective to develop and execute a framework for building and sustaining a civil workplace. The corporate approach to building a civil organization is centered on 1) Surveying and assessing the prevalence and impact of workplace incivility, 2) Building civility as a leadership behavior into your corporate strategy, 3) Introducing civility as a cultural norm to your workforce through keynote speakers, seminars, and presentations at small group and organization-wide events, 4) Developing and present experiential workshops to address and resolve group issues around workplace incivility, 5) Appoint and train civility ambassadors (practitioners) to help organizations and work groups build positive cultures, and 6) Develop individual and group executive coaching programs to address specific issues around deviant workplace behaviors.

Workplace Civility Matters© Program Overview

What To Do Next?

If you are feeling overwhelmed by new insights into workplace incivility and the various avenues to pursuing a civil workplace perhaps you need to just take a deep breath and then assess the lay of the land. Conduct your own assessment of your awareness of the deviant aspects of your workplace that contribute to workplace incivility, using the insights offered in Part One under the heading of *"Recognizing Acts Of Workplace Incivility"* then see how many of the 40 individual activities you can begin to practice from Part Two under the heading of *"Workplace Civility (The Antithesis Of Workplace Incivility)"*.

If however you want a more concrete plan for your organization then let us deliver the Workplace Civility Assessment Survey (WCAS) to your team, workgroup, or organization and together we can measure the extent to which incivility appears to be a problem, and then assess your employees' propensity for developing and sustaining workplace civility as a cultural norm. You can then employ the results of the comprehensive survey to develop an organizational-wide civility response mechanism, towards establishing civility as a cultural norm while positively impacting organizational performance and business outcomes. We are just an e-mail away…. INFO@WorkplaceCivilityMatters.com

Welcome.....I Am Dr. Martina Carroll-Garrison
I Build Cultures Where Workplace Civility Matters©

- After 25 years of Federal Service with DOD and FBI I
  - reinvented myself as a Georgetown trained and ICF certified
    - Executive Coach,
    - Corporate Trainer,
    - Management Consultant,
    - Adviser and Mentor and
    - Public Speaker!

- My niche in coaching high performing individuals and organizations
  - including STEM community

Who Am I?